Mary Kyle Dallas

The freed spirit

Glimpses beyond the border

Mary Kyle Dallas

The freed spirit
Glimpses beyond the border

ISBN/EAN: 9783337120399

Printed in Europe, USA, Canada, Australia, Japan

Cover: Foto ©Thomas Meinert / pixelio.de

More available books at **www.hansebooks.com**

THE FREED SPIRIT

OR

GLIMPSES BEYOND THE BORDER

A COLLECTION OF NEW AND AUTHENTIC OCCULT TALES
FROM THE AUTHOR'S PERSONAL EXPERIENCE
AND RELIABLE PRIVATE SOURCES

BY

MARY KYLE DALLAS

Author of "The Devil's Anvil," "The Grinder Papers," "The Nine Iron Bars," etc

NEW YORK
CHARLES B. REED, PUBLISHER
164, 166 & 168 FULTON ST

1894

PREFACE.

Most writers begin a book of this sort by informing their readers that they are not spiritualists, or else, more rarely, that they *are*, and why.

Therefore, it appears that it is proper to classify one's self, and I should like to do it if I could; but the fact is I do not yet quite know what I believe, and I claim the right to change my opinions as often as I please.

What I believed five years ago, I do not believe to-day, and I dare say that if I am on earth five years from now, I shall have found reason to believe many other things which I now take *cum grano salis*.

Therefore, I am, dear reader, neither spiritualist nor skeptic. Regard me, if you please, as a story-teller, but one who is now, as she solemnly believes, telling you only true stories.

What I have experienced myself, I have not embellished in the least, and when I tell you what others have told me, it is because I positively believe that they told the truth.

At the end of the volume I have a few pages of mystery stories, which I simply introduce as curiosities, but when I say Mrs. A or Mr. B told me this, you may be sure that I thought those ladies and gentlemen spoke the truth as I listened to them.

I should be glad to use their names, but in most cases that has been forbidden, and I have been obliged to have recourse to the alphabet. You will, therefore, have to take my word for it that the heroes and heroines really live and move and had the experiences which are here set down.

* * * * * * * *

Psychical research has thoroughly sifted too many family ghost stories, and examined the proofs of too many prophetic dreams, to allow us to believe that they are all hallucinations.

If we accord any value to human testimony, we must believe—as I aver, without a blush, that I do—that at the solemn hour of death, the dying are, at times, permitted to visit those whom they love best; that "wonder-opened eyes have seen" the semblance of the forms of the departing, when their faint and exhausted bodies were lying motionless upon their pillows, when those about them thought them dead.

These tales are proven by the testimony of worthy people in their right minds, and can scarcely be doubted. Within an hour of the apparent death, men and women have seemingly stood before others at a distance. Usually they appear to wear the costume that they do wear at the time. Those who see them are generally alone and in a composed state of mind, oftenest reclining.

Moreover, there are people living who will assure you that they have actually left their bodies and found themselves in some place at a great distance, observing the events that there transpired, and have been able to describe everything accurately, and that people on the spot have afterward corroborated their statements.

These were persons upon whom the trance fell without warning, who were not seeking such a condition, but to whom it came as sleep does, or a swoon, without the intervention of another human being. These clairvoyants are always able to describe what they have observed. Their memory of words and deeds, of form and coloring, is vivid. What they·do not know, is how they came or went. They found themselves at a distant place, they find themselves again in the accustomed one without knowing how—that is all. It seems to them that they must have taken their bodies with them. But those who watch them, tell them that they have remained in the chair or upon the couch all the while, silent, motionless, apparently unconscious, often with the eyes wide open.

Certainly, if we are but once sure that the spirit can thus leave the living body, taking with it all that makes up the identity, we

need never succumb to the despair which those feel who believe that
"When we die, why, there's an end on't."

A queer sort of false pride makes many men pretend that they like that idea. But give them a little hope that it is a false one, and they rejoice more than those who have always been supported by faith.

However, we are all aware that such hopes are like vines—they need something to cling to, and not all need the same thing. The morning-glory asks only a little silken thread on which to climb heavenward, but you must give the ivy a rough stone wall.

For many a doubter, the proof that a living man can leave the body, and be a man for all that, would be a good, strong cord by which he could reach the heights where there are prospects of which those who linger in the valley do not know, and where he once more sees the sun, which seemed to him, down there below, to have set long ago.

I know of several such cases of clairvoyance, and they are proofs to me. Naturally, they cannot be as convincing to you, but I assure you that I will not, for the sake of making the stories better, add anything to them. So far you can trust me. And now, without further preface, I will tell you the most important clairvoyant story that I am able to relate, in full faith that it is perfectly true—that of Mr. Apell, a Scotch gentleman, residing, at the time, in the United States.

THE FREED SPIRIT

OR

GLIMPSES BEYOND THE BORDER

INDEX.

	PAGE.
CHAPTER 1.—Mr. Apell's Vision.	1
Mrs. G's Story,	8
Miss Annie Starbird's Story,	9
Told by Mr. John Garnis,	11
CHAPTER 2.—The Appearance of Departed Spirits,	13
My Grandmother's Ghost Story,	16
My Own Story,	26
CHAPTER 3.—Odd Happenings,	30
My One Song,	35
A Real "Grandfather's Clock,"	36
What Was It?	37
A Warning of Calamity,	38
Out of the Body,	39
CHAPTER 4.—Dopple Gangers,	42
An Apparition in Red, Blue and Yellow,	44
CHAPTER 5.—Somnambulism,	47
Mr. Alpheus Bixby,	48
Mrs. Brick's Dinner,	48
Miss Primula's Acrobatic Performance,	50
Above the Whirlpool at Midnight,	52

		PAGE.
CHAPTER 6.—Dreams,		54
My Sister's Dream,		56
My Mother's Dream,		59
A Neighbor's Dream,		60
The Persian Rug,		61
A Dream of the Fourteenth Century. The Finding of the Last Cantos of Dante's Divina Comedia,		62
CHAPTER 7.—Ghost Stories,		65
Mr. Blomgren's Call,		66
A Mississippi Pilot's Story,		67
Dr. F's Story,		71
What a Musician Saw,		72
The Ghost in the Back Parlor,		74
A Haunted Man,		77
CHAPTER 8.—A Covington Apparition,		84
A Reproachful Ghost,		85
A Sorrowful Ghost,		89
Poor Hannah Penny,		95
The Twins,		97
A Pretty Story of Helen Hunt Jackson,		98
CHAPTER 9—Nurse Kirkpatrick's Stories,		100
How a Spirit Sat for Its Photograph,		105
The Story of a Watch,		109
A Dream,		112
Sister Zelia,		113
A Virginia Witch Story,		115

INDEX.

| | PAGE. |

CHAPTER 10.—Three Celebrated Mediums:
    Miss Edmonds, - - - - 125
    Charles Foster, - - - - 127
    Mrs. Margaret Fox Kane, - - - 136

CHAPTER 11.—About Babies, - - - - 138
    A Baby Ghost-Seer, - - - - 143

CHAPTER 12.—Planchette, - - - - 144

CHAPTER 13.—Colonel Deyer's Well, - - - 150

CHAPTER 14.—The Story of Mrs. V, - - - 163
    Extract From a Letter, - - - 168

CHAPTER 15.—The Anxious Mother, - - - 171
    Two Pictures of Heaven, - - - 180
    The Case of Mrs. Roger Black, - - 183

CHAPTER 16.—Mediums of Uncivilized Nations:
    The Kaffirs, - - - - - 188
    The Ashantees, - - - - 188
    The Dahomians, - - - - 189
    The Australians, - - - - 190
    The Maoris, - - - - - 193
    The Fijians, - - - - 194
    The Abyssinians, - - - - 195
    Spiritual Belief of the Esquimaux, - 197

CHAPTER 17.—Testimony From All Quarters, - - 201

	PAGE.
CHAPTER 18.—The Belief of Agassiz in the Eternal Continuance of Individual Personality,	211
Immanuel Kant on the Hope of Immortality,	211
Lord Byron on the White Lady of Colalto,	212
Mozart's Belief in Omens,	213
Mr. Frith's Dream of Dickens,	213
Victor Hugo,	213
Abercrombie's Opinion,	214
A Beautiful Hope of the Theosophist,	216
Herbert Spencer,	217
The Fathers of the Church,	217
Extracts from Hawthorne's Note-Books,	218
CHAPTER 19.—The Haunted Hearth,	220
Sleeping-car Dreams,	224
CHAPTER 20.—Mystery Stories,	228
The Son Restored to His Mother,	229
St. Luke, Chapter VII,	231

CHAPTER I.

MR. APELL'S VISION.

I believe that "Second-sight" was claimed by certain members of Mr. Apell's family, and that he himself had other experiences of the same sort. Be that as it may, on a certain day, many years ago, Mr. Apell was sitting with his wife in the room they usually occupied in the evening, talking of indifferent subjects, when he suddenly became silent.

Looking at him in some surprise, his wife saw that he was sitting in his arm-chair, on one side of the grate fire, in a rigid position, with his eyes wide open and fixed, as though they saw nothing. She had seen him in this state before, and had learned that it was best not to disturb him; that if no effort were made to arouse him, he would finally come to himself and suffer no more than a somnambulist does under the same circumstances. Therefore she wisely remained silent and went on with her sewing, as though nothing strange had occurred.

I do not remember how long Mr. Apell remained in that strange condition into which he had fallen, but it was a very long while for such a state to continue. When, at last, he began to move and once more to be conscious of his surroundings, he seemed very unhappy, both distressed and shocked; and, after rising and pacing the room for awhile, told his wife that he had just seen his father die, and was assured that he should soon receive news which would prove that he was not deceived by his imagination.

Mrs. Apell, who placed faith in the power of Second-sight, was naturally much affected by what her husband told her, but waited until he felt able to tell the particulars of his vision, which he shortly did.

He remembered saying something to his wife and hearing her reply die away in the distance, as it were, but he could not catch it or comprehend it. There was temporary oblivion, and then he found himself, in some strange way, at a political meeting in a place which I have forgotten, and in which his father was at the time residing. A great number of people had gathered, a platform had been built and he noticed certain favorite orators gathered upon it and heard them speak. He seemed, in fact, to be attending the meeting as he would in the ordinary way if he had been present in the body; recognized old friends, joined in the applause which followed the speeches, and had no odd sensations whatever; only no one spoke to him. Suddenly, he saw his father and a brother arrive upon the scene. They had evidently been belated, and the fact that his father was to speak from the platform was mentioned by those in the throng. His name was called and he ascended the steps, followed by his son. There was the usual hand-shaking and greeting; some one announced him, and he stepped forward. He opened his lips, appeared confused, uttered a few incoherent words and suddenly put his hand to his heart and fell backward—

Mr. Apell saw that it was into his brother's arms. A doctor was called for; one came from the audience. The invisible spectator saw all that was done in the effort to restore consciousness. Then he saw them bring his father down the steps. He heard the doctor declare that he was dead. He witnessed his brother's grief. Then he knew that they consulted as to the best way of conveying the body to its home, which was at some distance. The place was a rural one, not provided with all conveniences. There seemed to be no carriage to be had. Some amongst the number procured some plain pine boards, of which they hastily made a rude coffin. He heard all their remarks and the sounds of the tools they used. He saw them place his father's body in this box, and he saw them lift it into a wagon which was driven up.

"Brother Bob," he said, "was like one stunned. I never saw a man so dazed in my life. I wanted to rouse him, and I put my arm about him. He did not seem to feel me. 'Bob, my boy,' said I, 'this is a sad hour. We have lost a good father, and it will break mother's heart. I cannot fancy her living long without him.' But I could see that he neither heard nor felt me, that he did not know that I was there. I could not understand it; it seemed to me that I was exactly as I always was. I could look down and see my own figure and feel the cloth of the coat I wore, and when I put my hands together they felt as they always do. In a kind of horror, I turned and spoke to two or three others. They were all as deaf and blind to me as Bob had been. I saw Andrew Muir, whom I went to school with. I put out my hand and touched his. He began to rub his fingers, and whispered to some one that his hand tingled as if he had taken hold of an electric battery. After that I touched nobody, but I spoke to the doctor. 'Doctor,' said I, 'has my father been complaining? Was there any reason to expect this?' It was plain that he did not hear me either. I stood straight before him and he took no notice of me. It was a very terrible thing to bear; but I felt that I must stay and go with them to my mother, and try if I could comfort her a little, and I thought that I would ride in the wagon. I went toward it, and my foot was on the wheel, and that is the last that I remember." Then, he said, all vanished and he saw his own home, his wife sitting opposite him, all as it had been when that strange condition came upon him.

This and more he told, and waited for the news that he was sure would come.

It arrived in due time. All had happened exactly as in his dream. The people he had seen were there, each had played his part precisely as in the vision. The coffin had been made by the people he had seen make it, and of the wood he had noticed was used.

Mr. Apell had actually been on the spot—or, at least, that which was the man, that which thought and suffered, and commented and remembered.

Meanwhile, Mr. Apell's person, his legs, arms, ears and eyes, his flesh and blood, clad in its raiment of cloth and linen, sat in his chair at home. He was not dead—neither did he wear the aspect of death.

What he seemed to be, was asleep with his eyes open, only that he was more rigid than most sleeping folk.

Generally, in sleep, the head lolls, the mouth falls open, the limbs relax—yet not always. I have myself seen people sit bolt-upright and motionless, during a long nap.

Assuredly, if you do not disbelieve this tale, you will see that there is a possibility of the spirit—I know not what else to call it—leaving the body for a space, as one might leave one's house, and of returning to it afterward.

It may be that this is a matter quite disconnected with the existence of a spirit after death, that it does not prove immortality, yet I think that there is more to hang a hope upon in such an experience as this, than in seeing the likeness of one departed, with one's waking eyes.

Nature has made, in making the eye, a beautiful and wonderful thing, but it is liable to accident. It may repeat what it has once seen, it may distort what it looks upon, or multiply it.

The drunken man sees two lamp-posts, and between them falls to the ground, but in such a case as that just narrated, the eyes and ears were left behind, and yet there was vision, and words were heard. The brain was under Mr. Apell's hair, yet he thought, he felt, he drew inductions, above all, he had strong emotions. How did that happen?

What would have been the result, if, during that period of trance, some one had murdered the Mr. Apell who sat in his chair at home—cut off his head, stabbed him to the heart, made his body untenantable? Would he also have murdered the man who was at the political meeting, and who, later, was grieving over his father's death? Was this identity only part of the figure sitting by the fireside? I do not think so.

Of his departure or return Mr. Apell knew nothing; those moments were mere blanks. He was here—he was there; and there was no sense of time occupied in the change of place.

If *he* did not go and come, *what* went and came? I do not pretend to know. Call it a dream if you please, and then tell me what power painted that scene, those faces, moved them to do all that they did, repeated what they said with the accuracy of an audiphone? It seems to me, being so exact a record of events transpiring at the moment, so many miles away, to be as wonderful, if it were a dream, as in any other class of phenomena. But dreams generally have a hole in them somewhere. Even when "veridical," they are usually figurative and emblematic in a degree, or they have absurd points, only known to be so when the dreamer wakens.

Mr. Apell's description of the scene at his father's death was that of an eye-witness. Very few reporters stick as close to facts; very few persons who appear upon the witness-stand are as accurate. Well-meaning people will say that a man exclaimed "My goodness," when he cried out "Good Heavens"; that he struck another with a cane, when he really used an umbrella; or that he threw a brick, when he really threw a stone.

Mr. Apell, according to the account which I have always relied upon as truthful in every particular, made not one mistake of this sort.

And now one asks one's self: which was the real Mr. Apell all this while? His body, arrayed in its accustomed manner, was at his own fireside. His wife saw it; it was her husband, and it was not her husband. That which we value in our friends had left it; it had no consciousness, no interest in her. Whatever had happened to her, he would have taken no heed of it.

The presence of his form was of no value; it was simply a semblance of him as a statue might have been, no more.

His spirit was far away, amidst the scenes he afterward described. He witnessed his father's death with the same distress that he would have felt had he had his body with him, sympathized with his brother and with those of his kindred whom the sad news would shock, and bethought him of his wife as at a distance, and of her feelings when she should be told of what had happened.

Was not that the man whom his wife loved—who loved her? If by some accident the body in the chair had been made untenantable, would that have done away with the identity?

Unless that story is false, can you say that it does not prove that the body is nothing but a coat, which we wear and cast away when we have done with it? That it is true, and that hundreds like it are also true, it would be actual folly to doubt because you may never have been clairvoyant, or had an opportunity of observing a case of the sort. You do not deny that the Atlantic cable is in existence, because you have never sent a message across it.

8 THIS STORY IS ANOTHER OF THE SAME ORDER.

As I have not asked permission of the lady I shall now speak of to use her name, I will only call her Mrs. G.

She was a very young woman at the time, and was also very, very ill. She lay in her bed in the second floor of a house in Greenpoint, L. I., and had proved by various remarks that she had a strange power of seeing things not within the range of her vision—a power she did not possess at other times.

About eighteen years have gone by since that day when she suddenly opened her eyes and told those about her that she had just seen a young man they all knew (a neighbor who was on the police force) murdered.

I think that a heavy stone was thrown at him, but certainly she saw him stagger against a wall and fall, dying.

The young man's name was Phelps—my impression is that the whole name was William Phelps—but he lived with his family, who were very fond of him and very much attached to each other, and were very near neighbors of the sick lady.

At this time they were occupied in their usual way, and had evidently heard no ill news, and no one attached any importance to the dream; but, a few hours later, one came bringing the bad tidings. The young policeman had been engaged in assisting to quell a riot, and one of the rioters had killed him. Exactly as my friend had seen him in her dream, he had staggered against a wall. Just as she had described, and, certainly, in the same hour that she had seen him die, he had really done so. During this lady's illness, I was told, she could see persons who rang the door bell and tell who desired admittance, or, if anything were lost, could direct others where to find it.

I saw none of this, but have every reason to believe that the facts were as stated.

MISS ANNIE STARBIRD'S STORY

Seems naturally to follow this one. Again the seer gained the power of clairvoyance in illness, and lost it during health.

She was, at the time, a young lady of twenty, and her dwelling place was a country house in the State of Maine. Her name was Annie Starbird.

Having taken too long a walk, a peculiar illness overtook her. She was quite well so long as she lay upon her back; but if she tried to sit up, she fainted away. In this illness her mother cared for her, and it soon became a common thing for the daughter to foretell events, ordinary things of no special import, but always "coming true," and thus taking upon themselves an interest they would not otherwise have possessed.

One, which she told me, I remember in detail.

Her aunt and cousins were coming to dine and spend the day. They would come in their own vehicle, and were expected to arrive so that the meal could be partaken of between noon and one o'clock. During the morning, Annie called her mother and said:

"If you want dinner to be hot when auntie comes, mother, you will have to put it off until three o'clock.

I have just seen auntie and cousins. They started so as to be here in good time, but (at such and such a place—mentioning it by name) the wagon broke down. It is a serious accident, though no one is hurt. One of them "—mentioning the person by name—" was obliged to go a long way to get some one to do repairs. Then the work itself will take a long while. They know they cannot get here before three o'clock and are very sorry. Every one is doing all that can be done, but there is no such thing as hastening matters," and she described the injury to the wagon and what the smith was doing.

Mrs. Starbird had such faith in the clear-seeing of this invalid daughter, that she took her advice. Dinner was postponed until the hour mentioned, or even a little later, and the guests enjoyed it in due season. It was just ready when they arrived.

The accident had happened exactly as Annie had described it. And the long walk, the discussion, the slow operations of the smith, and the particular portion of the wagon injured, were all as they were seen by Annie and described to her mother. With her, the things seemed to be seen in a dream.

Afterward, on her recovery, the lady grew healthy and stout, and saw only as others do. She was eminently practical, it appeared to me, and one of the last people of whom one would expect anything abnormal. Poor Annie! it is now many years since

"Death hath taught her more
Than this melancholy world doth know—
Things greater than all lore."

I fancy that she was glad to find herself a free spirit.

There are some in New York who will remember this lady tenderly, and know that one may rely upon a statement made by her. She taught here, and in Bath, Long Island, and was also an art-student in this city some years after she had these strange clairvoyant experiences. It was then that I had the pleasure of her friendship, and she told me these occurrences.

TOLD BY MR. JOHN GARNIS.

One of the friends of our family was Mr. John Garnis. I believe he was well known as a prominent business man in Cincinnati. He was very intelligent and a person who was not easily to be imposed upon. He had made a fortune, kept a bright lookout in every direction, and said just what he meant on all occasions.

I remember when I was about nine years old that he called on my grandmother, as he was in the habit of doing every time he came to the city, and began to tell a story of a clairvoyant to whose rooms a friend had recently taken him.

He said that he thought of his wife whom he had left in another city—Philadelphia, I believe—and the clairvoyant went into the trance state and declared that he had found her. He described her as an unusually large, tall lady, as she was, in deep mourning, and said that she was superintending the moving of the family belongings into a new house. Mr. Garnis knew that this was to be done shortly, but did not believe that the dwelling was yet ready for occupation. However, he asked the clairvoyant to describe the house. He at once said that it was built of red marble. Mr. Garnis tried to make him believe himself mistaken. But he insisted on the red marble, which was really the material that had been used. He also said that a very large mirror had been injured, or was likely to be, I forget which, but at the moment there was great excitement in regard to such a glass. He saw a desk brought in and described it; and on this, Mr. Garnis had asked him to see if there was a letter in the drawer of this desk, and, if so, to read it. He asserted that he did so. It was an ordinary business letter, *but he gave its whole contents and the signature.*

There was more that I have lost from my memory, but Mr. Garnis said that he wrote home at once, found that his wife had moved on that very day and that the statement in regard to the mirror was correct. He had known before that the house was of red marble and that the contents of the letter had been given correctly.

CHAPTER 2.

THE APPEARANCE OF DEPARTED SPIRITS.

Those who, as yet, have lost no dear one, are apt either to laugh at " a ghost," as something " funny," or to feel a profound repugnance to the subject. That is quite right and wholesome, as it is perfectly natural. While all we love still live, why should we think of the dead ? Most very young people have a curious feeling toward those who have lost many friends. They cannot understand, as they do in later years, that this is the common lot, and that none escape it, save by dying in their youth : they feel as though the mourners were specially set apart.

How well I remember saying to myself—" If those I love should die, I should surely die too," and believing that people on whom such blows fell must be specially made to endure them ; that they could not love their parents, their brothers and their sisters as I did, and still go on eating and drinking and sleeping and even taking some comfort in life. The dead are other people's dead in those glad times, and we only wish not to think about them. And then, though we usually hear about another world in Sunday-school and church, and, in a sort of general way, expect to go to Heaven, we do not ask ourselves much about that either ; still less, perhaps, in those years when childhood has passed, and the day of dreams has come. Neither poet nor preacher can paint a paradise more perfect than the gardens of delight we find on earth while love and hope walk hand in hand with us, under youth's blue skies, beside sweet fountains and amongst the roses. And such joy may remain with the wife and mother for long years, so that every night she thanks Heaven that she lives.

But one day the shadow of death crosses the threshold of the little home. "*One is taken and the other left.*" If the one who is left be the woman, fiends might pity her, for the earth becomes a desert, and all that made it beautiful vanishes thence. The brighter life has been in the past, the deeper is its darkness now.

"Weary, stale, flat and unprofitable," seem to her, "all the uses of the world."

There is nothing worth doing, or having; nothing worth living for—and oh, the astonishment, the awful surprise of it, the difficulty of believing that this can really have happened!

It has seemed as if Heaven smiled on such innocent happiness as that of home love; as if God had given a promise of its continuance because it was so sweet and holy, and all the while (it appears at this moment to the wretched mourner) He did not care. How many a young widow has felt, in her desolation, that she was deserted by the Heaven in which she had put her trust! More than ever, when the first hours of passionate lamentation passed, the woeful time comes when she knows that she must go on living without *him*, when the thought, best conveyed in Mrs. Browning's words:

> "The heart which, like a staff, was one
> For mine to lean and rest upon;
> The strongest on the longest day,
> With steadfast love—is caught away,
> And yet my days go on, go on."

is with her always.

Nor is it only the widow who feels thus, but any one of two who have lived in perfect affection and confidence together, mother and child, brother and sister, or sometimes two who are not kindred, save in soul.

Now, indeed, the mourner begins to ponder on another world than this, to ask herself if, in the beyond, they twain may not meet again. It is all she cares for now. All the blue has gone out of the sky, all the sweetness out of the flowers, all is cold and harsh that once was soft and pleasant. Wealth would be valueless—for I am not talking of widows who are comforted by being "left well off," or of kindred who find satisfaction in inheriting real estate or portable property; but of those to whom love was life—and all the rest only of value because it could make the dear one's days brighter—the woman to whom a new dress or a bright ribbon, a rose in the belt, or a jewel at the throat, were not mere tributes to vanity, but valued only as they made her fairer to her beloved; and of the man who rejoiced in a beautiful home, because his dear ones dwelt within its walls; in a full purse, because it enabled him to gratify the wishes of those dependent on him. For such, for all who have adored and lost, life's day is at an end forever when the well-beloved has passed beyond his ken. May it not be that the Omnipotent has now and then permitted the curtain to be lifted, the gate to be left ajar, that through them, illuminating the darkness of the gloomy night, may shine the light of one soft star, or that, listening intently, they may hear the angels whisper—"Have courage, the pure in heart shall meet again."

If for such purpose the spirit is permitted to linger, or to return, who shall scoff at those who open their arms in welcome?

For my part, I am quite sure that in the dying hour, adieux may be given. One proof that I have of this is a story that has gone with me all my woman's years, a tale I cannot doubt, because no false word ever fell from the lips that uttered it. It is neither more nor less than what I call it—my grandmother's ghost story.

MY GRANDMOTHER'S GHOST STORY, AND MY OWN.

Lest you should fancy my grandmother a superstitious old lady, fond of curdling the blood in people's veins with tales of the ghostly sort, I must tell you first that she was a gentlewoman of high social position, a beauty in her youth, the centre of a literary circle in her prime, when people knew her as a writer of poems and sketches, and, all her life, a bright, sensible and eminently practical woman, who never told ghost stories, and, though she penned many tales, never wrote one in which a spectre figured.

Yet, this is her ghost story; I have added nothing to

it, I have subtracted nothing from it. She never told it to a stranger and she never told it to me until I was fifteen years old, when my mother informed me that grandma had once had a strange experience, which I might persuade her to relate.

I shall never forget the expression that crossed her face as she yielded to my persuasions. I wish I could tell it in her own words; I wish I could bring her dear face before you as it rises before my memory at this moment. The tone, the look were convincing, and would be enough for me, but proofs in black and white existed, and may yet exist, for all I know, that established the tale as "veridical." My grandmother was born in Newport, in the day when Malbone painted his first miniatures there, for he painted little Harriet with flowers in her tiny hands. Her mother was a daughter of Colonel Belcher, who was an officer of the English army. Her father was a Frenchman, who, in a romantic spirit, relinquished a title when he became a resident of the United States, preferring the Republican prefix, Mr., especially as he had entered into business. The little home was a very happy one. The parents were young, her father very merry, and light-hearted.

Colonel Belcher had already passed away when little Harriet came to her seventh year, and Mrs. Belcher had come to live with her daughter. My grandmother remembered her as large and stately, wearing a profusion of snow-white hair, combed up over a cushion, and brocaded gowns that would stand alone when placed upon the floor, so rich was their material.

Her daughter, however, was delicate as a flower, sensitive and emotional. She adored her husband, who was devoted to her, and lived only to be loved and petted.

Young as she was, my grandmother could remember her father's return from several voyages, which he made in connection with his business. His voyages were mostly to India, she believed. He always returned in high spirits, laden with presents for every one, and for days afterward there was nothing but feasting and merriment. Hosts of friends were entertained; it was a time of music, dancing and congratulations. The mother seemed to become herself a child again. But when once more Mr. Geoffroi spoke of making another voyage, she became depressed. "Life was unendurable without her Andrew," she often declared. At last came a time, when, having made every arrangement for one of his departures, the young husband was about to say adieu to his wife. He had already put his arm about her waist and bent his head to meet her lips, when she flung herself upon her knees before him, and clasping her hands, cried in frantic tones, "Ah! Andrew, do not leave me; if you do, you will never see me again. This is no fancy, I *know* it! If you go now, we part forever! You must not, you *shall* not make this voyage!"

My grandmother could remember how this affected her father, how he knelt beside his wife; how he took her in his arms and held her to his bosom. He was so deeply impressed that, had it been possible, he would have remained at home, but it appeared to him that it was impossible. His luggage was already on board, he had entered into certain contracts, and was in honor bound to do certain things.

"I must go this time, dearest," he said, "but I promise to make no more voyages. Others shall attend to my affairs; I will never leave you again. When I come home I will stay with you, I swear it."

All that the poor wife could do was to weep and to repeat, "I shall never see you again, Andrew! never!" And when at last their lips met in the final kiss, she whispered:

"This is our eternal adieu"—and fainted away.

For his part, Andrew Geoffroi departed sobbing, as one leaves the grave of a loved one. His thought was that this excitement might prove too much for the delicate woman he adored, and for whom there was special reason at the time to feel anxiety.

He had no fear for himself. "The sea and I are friends," he had often declared, "and I am never happier than when afloat."

This time, however, he sailed with a sad heart, longing only for the hour that would bring him home again.

For a few days Mrs. Geoffroi was ill, then she said no more of her presentiment; the child thought she had forgotten it.

My grandmother remembered every incident of that night in early autumn, a time of special beauty in Newport, when she followed her mother up-stairs to bed. It was about nine o'clock; they kept early hours then, and especially just at that time.

The tall clock, with the great, moon-like pendulum,

and big weights, and the ship that rocked on mimic billows, had sounded at the same time as the "nine o'clock bell," which sent young folks home from their parties, so that very particular folk were spoken of as "Tied to the Bell Rope."

Patience, the maid, in cap and apron, lit them with a tall candle; little Harriet clung to her mother's hand, which was put out behind her, in a pretty, girlish way she had.

When they went into the bed-room, Patience lit the two candles on the dressing-table, and drew the window curtains carefully.

In those days a bed-room was a solemn affair, with massive chests of drawers, dressing-tables, with draped glasses, deep arm-chairs and tall foot-stools. The bed was very large and wide, a pile of feathers, with bolsters, pillows, many blankets and wonderful quilts. Four tall posts arose to the ceiling, between them a canopy was stretched, and from this curtains depended on all sides. The legs of the bedstead were so long that its occupant ascended to it by a set of steps, and it had a "valance," ruffled and edged and otherwise decorated.

When her father was away, little Harriet slept in her mother's room, in a curious piece of furniture of the day called a trundle-bed, a little thing on wheels, which was pushed under the great bed during the day and drawn out at the foot at night. Patience now pulled this bed forward, and proceeded to brush her lady's hair, untie her slippers and unlace her stays.

Then, having undressed the child, she left them for a

little to their prayers and returned to complete her duties, one of which was "tucking in" the quilts of both beds, a high art of those days. Then she drew her lady's bed-curtains, leaving a space opposite the steps open, so that the great bed took upon itself the appearance of a house with a door, the child thought. Said "Anything more, Ma'am?" And being told that there was nothing, blew out the candles on the dressing table, took her own and went into the adjoining room, where she herself slept, and shut the door. The large apartment was now totally dark; not as much as a beam of starlight stole through the window curtains; nothing in the room was visible. My grandmother was sure that she was asleep in less than five minutes.

Usually she slumbered soundly until the morning. On this occasion she started wide awake with a consciousness of very novel sensations. She was intensely cold and extremely thirsty. All through her limbs ran curious thrills, which she long afterward learned were similar to those produced by the electric battery of the physician, then unknown to any one.

Something seemed to be combing her curls, separating every individual hair and lifting it straight up from her head. She longed for a glass of water and tried to call Patience to bring her one, but she had no voice: it was entirely gone. She strove to rise, but could not stir, and then, to her joy, she saw a light begin to grow in the room.

"Patience must be coming with a candle," she said to herself, but no Patience appeared, nor was the glow that of a candle; it was delicately but decidedly blue, it filled the whole room and revealed every object, but was brightest where the curtains were parted, and the child could see her mother's head upon the white pillow. At this instant the clock in the hall below struck twelve. At the last stroke, without having seen how he came or whence, she perceived her father standing in this bright space, looking down upon her mother.

He was clad in a long, white dressing-gown, about his head was fastened a white bandage, and he was very pale. At first his profile was presented to her, but in a little while he turned his head, his eyes met hers and he smiled, but very sadly. Then he did not "go" or fade away, he simply was not there. The light went out and all those curious feelings departed from the child's frame and she was her little, warm, comfortable self again and not in the least frightened.

She was only seven years old, had never heard, read or thought of the supernatural, and what she believed was that her father had returned after they were all in bed, that he would not awaken her mother, of whom he was always considerate, but that by way of jest he had pulled her hair and made her feel strangely. It troubled her to think that he must have hurt his head. Still she had once "bumped" her forehead and grandma cured it readily with her ointment. And happy to know that papa had come home, and with visions of the pleasant morrow in her mind, the child went to sleep again, but not at once, she was too thoroughly awakened and excited.

Early in the morning, she opened her eyes once more, jumped out of bed, and began to run from room to room in her little, bare feet, looking for her father. Coming to her grandmother's room, she begged to be told where she could find her father, and at first refused to believe that he was not in the house or that she had only dreamed that he was there.

"It was not a dream," she declared, "I was wide awake and saw him, grandma."

The grandmother turned pale, and very, very grave at this. She took from her work-bag a pocket-book she always carried, and wrote down the date, the fact that the child had heard the clock strike twelve, and all the particulars of the story. Then she charged her not to tell her mother of this dream, "for it must be a dream, child," she said, "since nothing of the sort has happened, and your mother is not very well and might be frightened." And though little Harriet repeated "dreams are not like that," she obeyed her grandmother.

The two now had a secret between them, and the old lady waited with terrible anxiety for news of the vessel in which Andrew Geoffroi had sailed, anxiety which finally communicated itself to the little girl.

Well did she remember how their hopes arose when the ship came into port at last. But alas, it did not bring Andrew Geoffroi. His wife's presentiment was not meaningless—he returned to her no more in this world.

It was a story common enough in that day. In mid-ocean a mutiny had broken out on board, soon quelled and with little loss of life. Its ringleaders lay below in chains; but alas! at its outset, a drunken wretch had broken open the door of Mr. Geoffroi's state-room, mistaking it for that of the captain.

Unaware of the disturbance, he was sitting at his table, writing a letter to his wife. He wore a white dressing-gown. The wretch struck him a blow with a handspike, cleaving his skull. When the ship's surgeon had bound the wound with a white cloth, it was exactly midnight. At the last stroke of the hour the dying man opened his eyes and moaned:

"Ah God, if I could but see my wife once more— once more," and so breathed his last.

Who shall say his prayer was not answered, for the night was the night of his little daughter's vision, the hour was the hour. She had seen his head bound up and the wound was in his head. The bandage was white, what had been used was a linen towel. The robe she had seen on the figure was such an one as he wore as he sat writing in his state-room, and his last earthly words had been of his wife, his last wish to look upon her face again.

The facts were well attested. There was Mrs. Belcher's pocket-book, in which all the child had told her had been written down under the date of the dream, with the hour given. There was an official record of the events by the captain of the vessel, another by one of the officers, and the letter Mr. Geoffroi had just begun, dated, and containing an allusion to the lateness of the hour. These records were in existence for years, to prove my grandmother's story true.

The tale needed still another tragedy to complete it: the young wife died of a broken heart and little Harriet was left an orphan. However, she had an affectionate grandmother, and was happily married at sixteen. She became a widow early, married a second time, and again wore widow's weeds. The only one of her children who outlived babyhood was my mother.

Naturally, the affection between them was intense; they never parted from each other. My grandmother lived with my mother after the latter was married and was as dear to us as she was.

We all looked up to her, and, from old habit, my mother never did anything of importance without taking wise counsel of my grandmother. Every one loved her, and people seldom get more love than they deserve in this world. My father gave her all the affection of a true son, and she often said that she loved him as well as she did her own child.

After her death, we all felt for years as though she were still with us and we had told her everything and knew what she thought about new acquaintances whom she had never seen, and once, while my father, mother and myself were sitting before the fire, this happened:

The door of grandmother's room opened, her step fell on the floor, we heard the sound of her hand as she rested it on the edge of a piece of furniture to support herself (for she had been feeble for some time before she passed from among us), just as though we had been sitting in the dark and had heard her enter.

My father had an actual scorn of superstition, but it was not only I and my mother who breathed my grandmother's name, he uttered it also. What he said was: "My God—that is mother."

He spoke in solemn and reverential tones. Then we sat quietly, holding each other's hands for many minutes, and never afterward alluded to the experience. But it was positive, a thing to remember while one lived, as I shall.

That was long ago; I have never heard her since, but I have seen her.

MY OWN STORY.

In the month of September, 1885, my mother was living and, seemingly, in good health, and likely to live for many years longer.

We had for three summers occupied a house at Mianus, a little Connecticut village, not far from Cos-Cob station, and were staying later than usual.

I had been out for a walk one pleasant afternoon, and had come home to find my mother reading in the dining-room. My sisters went up-stairs, but I sat down upon a lounge in the room, and, feeling curiously lazy, stretched my feet out, shut my eyes and instantly fell asleep. I have never known myself to sleep so soundly in the day-time, and it was unusual for me to take that sort of nap. When I awoke it was still a warm, bright twilight.

I lifted myself on my elbow and looked about the room and noted several things. Particularly that while I slept, the new servant had been setting the tea-table without awakening me by the necessary clatter.

As I thought of this, the girl brought in two plates of bread, and I noticed that she had arranged the slices in a very pretty way, the edges overlapping and turned inward, and I saw that everything she had placed on the table was arranged with geometrical precision, and said to myself "she is neat," and felt the usual satisfaction in thinking this of a newly hired domestic.

I tell you this that you may know I was wide awake, for afterward I found that all was just as I saw it then.

Meanwhile, I noticed that my mother sat in a small carpet-chair, quite unemployed, which was unusual for her, for she generally had a book in her hand, if she were not otherwise busy. "Somehow," I thought to myself, as the girl left the room, "mother does not look as she usually does." I had never perceived that there was any resemblance between my mother and grandmother, except the color of their eyes, but now my mother's features seemed the counterpart of grandma's. The sudden and perfect likeness startled me; and again, my mother never wore a cap: her hair, still black, though mixed with gray, was worn as she had worn it for long years. Now it was smoothed back beneath a little lace cap, with white satin ribbons, and she had on her shoulders a silk shawl of a soft cream color. I had never known mother to wear such a shawl.

In face, pose of the figure and every item of the dress, she had suddenly become the very counterpart of grandmother—and what was she looking at so wistfully?

I followed the direction of the dark eyes, and saw, at the other end of the long table, my mother, her head bent over the last page of a book which she was intent on finishing before the light faded. Utterly absorbed in it, she noticed nothing else; it was her way when a book pleased her.

The difference in the two faces was more marked than I had thought it.

"It was Grandmother"—I said, under my breath—"Grandmother."

I looked back again at the little carpet-chair, but it was empty. I arose and went out into a place we called the grove; there I walked up and down, saying to myself: "after twenty years I have seen her again, after twenty years I have seen her." I had no doubt whatever about it, it was as if one I knew to be alive had come and gone in that strange way. I had been no more excited than I should have been in meeting a living friend so dear as she had been, after so long an absence.

Whatever it was, it was no dream. I said to myself over and over again, "After twenty years I have seen her again," and the impression made upon my mind was that wherever she dwelt her thoughts were with us still, her tenderness yet ours. The look she had fixed upon my mother was a very earnest one, and I remembered that old belief—the superstition of the peasant everywhere—that when the spirit of a mother is seen looking at a son or daughter, it is because death is close at hand.

I tried to drive the thought away, but it remained with me, although, at the time, my mother was in excellent health and spirits and showed few signs of age, and there was no special reason for anxiety.

I never told my mother of this happening, nor my other relatives, until afterward.

In November, my mother was suddenly taken ill and died after a few weeks' illness, and, in my sorrow, I confess that the memory of my vision has sometimes comforted me, for though others may believe it an hallucination, I have never been able to consider it one, and it is sweet to think that those two are together, and that mother-love is eternal.

CHAPTER 3.

ODD HAPPENINGS.

Curious things continually occur in commonplace households which are whisked away out of sight because there seems to be no place for them, nothing for them to stand on. The good housekeeping—so to speak—of certain orderly minds, consigns to the "trash-barrel" or the "rubbish-hole" everything that cannot be ranged neatly against its walls or hung upon them in geometrical order.

When a member of a family with minds of this sort has an unaccountable experience, and relates it, the general verdict is that "John is mistaken," or "Susy could not have seen straight," or "Sarah must have been dreaming."

Sarah knows she did not dream. Susy saw as she always did, and John knows that he made no mistake; but it is not worth while to argue, nor wise, if they wish to keep a reputation for common-sense. In such a household, a good, old-fashioned ghost, resembling the ironing-board that "came out of a dark corner" and "scared Susy half to death," would be more readily accepted than what one might call fragments of the occult.

But there are others who gather up these things and store them away and ask what they mean, and asking, find that they at least mean something and are glad to have it in their mental collection, just as some men rejoice in a broken bit of sculpture with certain signs about it which would be scornfully thrown away by the majority, who do not see the tokens that they bear.

Before many years more, regard will be paid to the singular little symptoms of the fact that the spirit of man has certain powers of which, as yet, we have not become aware.

I knew a lady, who, while dressing her hair in rather a cold room, felt and saw that her dressing robe was unfastened at the throat, the button having been wrenched off by the laundress.

Her neck and bosom were thus partially uncovered, but she looked in vain for a pin, there was none to be found. Therefore she went on with her hair, leaving her robe as it was; she was not at all nervous about herself or fearful of catching cold. Suddenly a thought from some other person came to her.

Not her own thought, as she says she was " spoken to, and not spoken to "; there was no audible utterance. Something gave her these words, as it were, within herself:

"You will have pneumonia, as I did." The image of a pleasant friend, who had recently passed away with the disorder mentioned, occurred to her mind, and she said to herself:

"If I believed in spirits I should say that the dear soul had tried to give me good advice—and I must take heed of it." And so, without more delay, she turned toward the door of an adjoining room where she was sure to find a pin-cushion, when she found that her robe *was* fastened carefully and neatly pinned across the bosom.

She will swear that she could find no pin, that her hands were above her head when those words of warning came to her, and that she saw herself reflected in the mirror before which she stood, with her sack wide open. As she turned away it had been fastened, and with peculiar accuracy. Of course, common-sense says a lapse of memory, she found a pin and forgot finding it, but my friend was very, very sure that this was not so.

This is the sort of thing that it is very hard not to believe a delusion. The ordinary spiritualistic idea of it would be, that the spirit stood unseen beside the lady and pinned her sack; but there is another idea, it is this—the thought of the spirit may have been powerful enough to have caused the sack to be fastened. That seems at first a wilder idea than the other. A Theosophist could put it into better form: there are words for everything of the sort in Theosophy, but I dare not use them because I only partially know what they mean, and I might not use them quite correctly, or if I did, you might never have heard them before.

People are apt to say to themselves that it does not matter what they think, if only their actions are all right.

It would be well if children were oftener taught to watch their thoughts, to try to think kindly of every one. A thought may be a blessing or a curse. Who would not shudder at the idea of being cursed aloud in solemn form? The curses only thought are just as fearful. People of whom others think in wrath and hate are conscious of it, sometimes, and a loving thought from afar may become almost palpable. Lovers know that.

Two people, absolutely in love, are aware of facts about each other that they have no means of knowing, save that their thoughts meet. They can say things to each other, though they are half ashamed to believe it, if they are educated people, and naturally do not tell any one about it. When married people remain true to each other, this power grows more intense; I have seen it exemplified twenty times.

Once, I remember, one of my sisters said to me:

"I have the funniest fancy just now. It seems to me that Charley (her husband) is playing with a little black dog."

When Dr. H—— came home a few hours after, he began to tell a story of a queer little black dog that came up to him in the street, leaped upon him and would not be driven away.

Therefore, though I have only read what follows in a daily paper, I give it credence. It is what I suppose the "rapport" of living married folk will ultimately result in.

It is a story of one married couple who declare that they have discovered that they can communicate their thoughts without using pen and ink, no matter how far apart they may be. The man is a commercial traveler.

Wherever he is, he goes at a certain fixed hour to his room in the hotel at which he stops—ten in the evening, if I remember correctly—fastens the door and sits down in the dark, and, of course, entirely alone. At the same hour the wife goes to their ordinary sitting-room, shuts and locks the door, places a chair at the fireside, takes another opposite it, and sits quietly in the dark, just as he is sitting. In a few moments, to her appreciation and to his, he is there, in his chair opposite her. They do not speak, but by some species of mental telegraphy, he makes her aware of all that has happened to him, and she tells him everything that has transpired at home.

He declares that they can do it more thoroughly than by writing, and prefer it. There has never been a mistake made during several years, and the gentleman says that they discovered this power by accident.

And what is a letter? Only the feeble interpretation of our thoughts, ideas, emotions, into characters, which, one by one, we slowly place on paper. It is a happy and wonderful thing that we are able to bridge the distance between ourselves and our dear ones in this way, but what mistakes we may make when the same word means two things or the writer does not know how to spell. A certain poet tells us how, once, upon a time, the good angels took advantage of this, and helped a poor widow thereby.

For the miserly old landlord had sent word to her lawyer to "remit" her rent, in the sense of making her pay it at once, and the lawyer read it in the other sense, and so remitted it, and this remission filled the widow's heart with gratitude, which she poured out upon the head of the old miser, who had never given any one cause to thank him thus before, and could not forego the unaccustomed delight, and found his heart softened, so that all ended in a Christmas dinner at the widow's and the birth of generous intentions in the miser's soul.

But not always do good angels seize these opportunities, and a word misunderstood has been the cause of life-long quarrels between friends, and the parting of lovers.

If thoughts could meet, without the aid of pen, ink and paper, can you not see how much better it would be?—or even than speech, for few of us have perfect command of language, and we continually misunderstand each other. I think that we will communicate thus in the beyond.

But now I want to tell you of one or two other things that I know to be true, though I cannot explain them.

The first is about my song—my one and only song, which, curiously enough, I did not hear myself sing, and had to take as a fact on hearsay evidence.

MY ONE SONG.

It used to provoke me greatly, in my girlish days, that I could not sing. I would have resigned all other accomplishments if in place of them I could but have possessed a genius for vocal music. I always deluded myself with the idea that I should some day discover that every one had been mistaken, that at least I had "latent talent," and when I married I fancied my husband, who was apt to think that whatever I did was well done, would assure me that all I needed was study and practice.

Alas, for my hopes! Mr. Dallas had an unusually correct ear and was a fine judge of music, and he decided that I could not sing at all.

One night, however, he awakened me to tell me a wonderful tale.

I had been singing, not only correctly, but, he declared, "charmingly," and with all the little tricks of a professional vocalist.

I thought that he was joking, but he vowed that he was only uttering the simple truth. I was sitting up with my eyes shut and sang a song of three verses from beginning to end. Then I assumed an expression of deep content and laid me down again, and he aroused me to tell me of it.

I had not dreamed of singing, or of anything; I seemed to myself to have been wrapped in profound slumber.

I was quite sure then that I should find that I could sing next day, but I could not; it was just the same as before. I could only think that while the "I" that could not sing slumbered, the "I" that knew it could kept awake and gave a performance for its own benefit.

A REAL "GRANDFATHER'S CLOCK."

Mr. John H—— is the proprietor of a hotel, which is within New York City precincts.

With him has resided, until now, his father, who was a mechanician of repute. In the house—I believe in the family sitting-room—he had placed a clock of his own manufacture, which was the pride of his heart. It was always in perfect order, and the old gentleman invariably wound it himself. It was the reliable time-piece of the neighborhood, as well as a beautiful piece of workmanship.

One evening—Friday, November 18th, 1892, old Mr. H——, being in usual health, and having left the house to walk in the garden for a while—a tremendous whirr and crash startled every one in the room, and it was found that the famous clock had stopped as suddenly as if some violence had been done to it.

Naturally, the young people thought at once of their grandfather, and one remarked—"I wonder why grandfather stays so long?" And they began to look for him.

He was found upon the porch, and as they ran to his side, he breathed his last gasp. He was dying when his precious clock, the work of his own hands, and for which he felt a peculiar fondness—"stopped short, never to go again"—for the H—— family declare that no hand shall ever touch it more.

WHAT WAS IT?

A relative of mine, a gentleman of strong, good sense, and utterly opposed to everything that lovers of the mysterious best like to believe in, was once staying at a country boarding-house, and one night had retired, as usual, when suddenly the bed clothes were jerked from above him.

He supposed that some one was playing him a trick, and uttered some words to that effect, and arose to replace the coverings. Having done so, he lit a light, found that his door was locked, examined closets, looked under the bed and up chimney, and retired again.

Once more the same thing happened. Again he searched, examined the corners of the quilts and sheets, shut down the windows, which had been open, and composed himself to slumber. He was awakened by having the coverings all removed with extraordinary violence, and on examination, found them hurled across the room. Again he searched, went into the passage, opened the windows and looked out, examined the walls, the floor, the ceiling, and, on retiring, experienced the same annoyance.

At last he put out the light, got into bed and rolled himself in the coverings. He asserts that they were violently pulled, and that he used all his strength to hold his position, but did so and went to sleep.

The next day he examined the room carefully, but could find no hole or aperture anywhere. There was no trap-door in the ceiling or the floor, no one could have entered, and though the trick could be done with cords and fish-hooks, there was no way in which this could have been arranged that night. He, however, always declared that some human being had played a practical joke upon him.

My brother-in-law, Mr. Charles L. Hildreth, told me the incident I will now relate. It happened years ago, when his mother was a young woman, living at home with her parents.

She had retired to bed in good health and spirits and had fallen asleep, when she was awakened by a heartrending scream from the lower floor, and the next moment her mother's voice uttered the words—"quick! they have killed your father!—oh, your father!"

Trembling with horror, the daughter rushed into the passage, but the house was dark and silent, and when she reached her parents' room she found them both sound asleep. No one had called her, nothing had happened.

The illusion had been so perfect that she could scarcely credit the fact that it was one, and the next day there was some talk on the subject of what was supposed to be her dream, and when she retired she remarked that she hoped she would never have another so terrible.

However, she had slept but a little while, when a scream broke her slumber, and, as she lifted her head, she heard the same words—"they have killed your father!—oh, your father!"

Certain that this was only a repetition of the delusion of last night, she lay still, determined not to disturb the house again—but the screams continued, she heard the sounds of men's feet upon the stairs and the tumult of many voices.

This time it was no delusion whatever, her father had been killed by a drunken ruffian as he was returning to his home and had been brought back dead.

I have a friend who, after sitting at a table for some time, can always tell those who sit with her how any deceased person, whose name they write upon a paper, came to his end.

It is not guess-work, but quite a certain thing. I

heard her give the answer—"lost at sea," in reply to such a question concerning one of whom she knew nothing, whose name she had never heard before, and that without hesitation. In regard to the four persons whose names were given her that evening she made no mistake.

This lady tells a story in which she at least believes implicitly.

In her early girlhood, she had one evening been to a party and had had a very pleasant time, and returned home and retired, thinking of nothing but agreeable things.

She lay awake going over the incidents of the affair for some little while, but went sound asleep at last and awakened to find herself standing in the corner.

She fancied that she had risen in her sleep, but in a moment perceived that her body lay upon the bed, wearing its night dress and well wrapped up in the coverings.

At first she was not frightened, but felt unusually light and well and happy. It was really delightful to have such airy, pleasant sensations, to feel as if she could float or fly if she chose, but suddenly the thought came to her, that if her spirit had left her body and this were death, she would soon be obliged to go away. She did not wish to leave her beloved ones, nor was she weary of life. Then her death would occasion grief and trouble. She longed to return to her body again, and made wild efforts to do so. Finally she found herself suffering inexpressible agony in the effort to enter the silent frame lying so quietly upon the bed, her dear little body, which she began to feel that she loved, and as she says:

"I did it, I got back, but I suffered frightfully in doing so."

She positively declares that it was not a dream, but an actual experience, and in another case I have had the same thing told me, only that this lady, suffering from asthma, thought herself floating over her bed, saw the doctor, the nurse and other friends bending over her body, declaring that she was dead; tried to return and did so. However, being so ill, she could not be sure that she was not the victim of delusion, although it did not so appear to her at the time.

CHAPTER 4.

DOPPLE GANGERS.

The next event that I remember, which was out of the common, does not properly belong to any special order of mysteries. It was not a ghost, it was not a dream. The seer was not in a trance. It is really a case of what the Germans call the *Dopple Ganger*. If it proves anything, it is only that—"there are more things in Heaven and earth" than are dreamed of in any one's philosophy, and we all know that already, for every one who writes about the supernatural always quotes it in some portion of his article.

When my brothers were boys, a friend of theirs, whom I shall call Will, was paying them a visit.

It was evening and my eldest brother had gone out. My younger brother and William were in the parlor, playing some game of cards. I left them there and went up-stairs. As I passed the door of what we called the "boys' room," I saw the gas flaring at a great height, and stepped in to turn it down.

Then I saw some one lying fully dressed on a small single bed just below the gas jet. I thought my elder brother had come home, and said something to the effect that I was not aware that he had returned, and, as I spoke, saw that it was not my brother, but William, or, as we called him, Will.

It puzzled me to think that he had passed me in the hall without my being aware of it, and I went down stairs again.

There was Will playing cards with my brother, as I had left them.

I went up again, sure that my oldest brother had returned, went into the room, and saw what looked like Will again. I walked slowly forward and noticed that he lay with wide open eyes, perfectly motionless. The color of the cloth of his clothes was gray; I noticed his collar and cuffs, his tie. I saw that the tints of his hair were more vivid than in nature, that his cheeks and lips were bright as if painted, and that his eyes were the brightest blue. A painting so colored would have been criticised as unnatural.

I knew that I was the victim of some illusion, and I walked deliberately up to the side of the bed and put my hand upon the pillow. There was nothing there, nor did I now see anything. I went out at the door again, staid a moment in the entry, and, returning, saw the same figure in the same place.

This time it vanished before I reached the bed.

I repeated this three times. Finally, on entering the room, I saw nothing, and turning out the gas, went down to the parlor again.

A few weeks after this, a friend from Philadelphia visited us. One afternoon we were in the back parlor and she said to me:

" How long that friend of your brothers sleeps!"

"Do you mean Will?" I asked. " He is not in the house."

"He has been lying on the sofa in that room all the afternoon," she said; "I have seen him several times."

She added that he was lying very still. There was a certain nervousness in her manner that startled me.

I went at once into the room she had indicated, and found no one there, and no one had been there, but my friend could scarcely be brought to believe it.

AN APPARITION, RED, BLUE AND YELLOW.

We were living quite in the suburbs of New York once upon a time, when, one day, my sister Louisa, returning homeward some time in the forenoon, saw a buggy stop at the corner of our street and a gentleman alight therefrom, exchanging some adieux with a lady who held the reins, and who was gayly attired in a blue silk dress, a red shawl and a yellow bonnet with plumes.

In a few moments the lady drove rapidly away and the gentleman came toward my sister. He was elderly, with gray hair, and now she fancied that she recognized him as our family doctor. She bowed and waited for him to come up, but no sooner had she said "good-morning, doctor," than she discovered that she was mistaken.

This gentleman was not Dr. Van B——, but he had taken his place beside her and walked on toward the house. He apparently fancied that my sister was some one he knew, and soon disclosed the fact that he was the new minister who had just taken charge of a new church hard by, and was paying his first visits to his congregation.

During the walk there was no lady anywhere near them; indeed, no one whatever in the quiet street but a little boy. When they reached the house, the clergyman entered, as a matter of course, shook hands with me, and went on with his talk about the church, the improvements, the Sabbath-school, etc., evidently thinking that he was very cleverly concealing the fact that he did not know which members of his congregation he had called upon.

The call over, he took his leave, and my sister Julia came running down stairs to ask who had called. Louisa told her of the mistake she had made, and we were laughing over it when Julia asked who the gorgeous lady was.

"Oh, I did not ask," Louisa answered.

"But he must have introduced her," Julia said.

"No; she did not leave the carriage," Louisa answered.

"I mean the lady who called with him," said Julia. "I looked over the balustrades and saw her. She had a blue dress, a yellow bonnet and a red shawl."

We both declared that no one had entered the door but the old clergyman, and Louisa asserted that, though a lady in the costume Julia described was in the carriage, she had driven away, and the carriage had never been near enough to our house to be seen from the windows.

They compared notes, and their descriptions of the dress, the shawl and the bonnet and feathers tallied exactly, only Louisa could merely say that the shawl was large, and Julia saw that the point and its fringe swept the carpet as the lady walked. She was behind the gentleman in entering the front door and in passing into the parlor.

At the time we told this to no one, and never saw the lady again—at least in that brilliant costume, but we have always thought it a very curious occurrence.

CHAPTER 5.

SOMNAMBULISM.

I have not personally known anything of somnambulism, and I trust I shall never have any experience of it. But it is a very singular phenomenon, and proves that we have some power of seeing, hearing and thinking, sufficient to take care of ourselves while our ordinary senses seem wrapped in slumber. We have all heard the old stock story—used up by authors and playwrights long ago—of the somnambulist who robs himself in that state, hides his money and jewels in a secret place, usually a vault, knowing nothing of it in his waking moments, accuses innocent people of the theft, until, followed by a faithful friend, he awakens to find himself out of his bed, clad in his night-robe, and busy in the task of concealing his own property, whereupon he is overcome with astonishment, and bestows dowries and blessings on everybody.

This story had its origin in fact, an old nobleman being the somnambulist; and that in those days when people were hung for theft, so that his magpie work was no joke to those under suspicion.

There seems to have been more of this sort of thing in the past than in the present, yet there are plenty of somnambulists still. Sometimes they do useful, instead of mischievous things: As when they help themselves out of difficulties and dilemmas into which they have plunged during their waking moments.

Musicians have had this experience, and boys, writing their college valedictories. But the mathematician is the usual somnambulist. There are hundreds of cases on record in which he figures.

MR. ALPHEUS BIXBY,

A teacher in a school which my mother attended, used to tell his class this story:

When he was a student, and a very ambitious one, he one day found himself utterly unable to solve a difficult mathematical problem. He worked at it all day and he worked at it all the evening without conquering his difficulty, and as something depended upon his success, was not only provoked and mortified, but grieved that he should have failed to do what he had attempted. He went to bed in a most unhappy state of mind, but slept soundly—as he would have supposed, without stirring.

In the morning, when he awoke, lo! there, upon his table, lay the problem, accurately solved, perfectly copied, an excellent piece of work in every particular—and his own.

In his sleep he had easily accomplished that which he found impossible in his waking moments.

Domestic labor is not often attempted by the somnambulist, but a Mrs. Brick, whom I knew years ago, used to tell a somnambulistic story about herself, though she never called it by that name.

She was a famous housekeeper, and would have been very unhappy if anything had been out of order about her premises, which she not only swept and dusted in the morning, but often at night before she went to bed, as well. Her meals were carefully cooked, and it was her delight to have everything of the best.

She gave a great deal of thought to her dishes, and liked to devise new ones. She made and mended and patched, and darned, and ironed, and crimped the ruffles of the family wardrobe, and, in fact, was a model Yankee house-mother. Everything she did was well done, yet she was always anxious about everything until it was off her mind. This is her story:

Once, upon a time, she had invited a large party to dinner.

She wished everything to be particularly nice, and had all the poultry, meat, vegetables, and other things necessary, already in the house. She was up rather late, and retired, thinking of dinner—that was all she knew about it.

Far on in the night, even in the small hours after twelve, Mr. Brick awakened to find his wife's pillow empty. At the same time he discovered that the house was redolent of the smell of cookery. It was not, by any means, time for breakfast, and his nose informed him that the odor was not that of the usual morning meal, but of one of Mrs. Brick's best dinners. There is a great difference, you know, between the smell of breakfast and of dinner.

Astonished beyond expression, he arose and partially dressed himself, went softly down stairs, saw that his kitchen was quite dark, except where the light of the stove illuminated it.

A bright fire was glowing, and cooking was evidently going on.

In haste he lit a lamp, and behold—his wife sitting bolt upright upon her chair, with her eyes partially open, but evidently asleep. In this state, she had arisen, dressed herself, gone into her dark kitchen, lit a fire and cooked one of the very best dinners of her life—which was saying a good deal.

She had not made a mistake, and when, a few moments later, she awakened, her astonishment knew no bounds. She had not the slightest consciousness of anything that had occurred since she had turned her head for the last time upon her pillow, having decided that hard sauce would be best for the pudding next day, and so feeling free to go to sleep again.

I find one other record of somnambulism upon my list. Here it is:

MISS PRIMULA'S ACROBATIC PERFORMANCE.

Miss ——, a maiden lady of very correct deportment, who belonged to a family remarkable for its serious views of life, and its dislike of anything like a joke, kept house for her bachelor brother in the old family residence in —— street. The other sisters were married and away, or had passed from earth, and Miss Primula—as I shall call her—ruled the establishment, and Mr. Joshua as well.

Two or three old servants went through the regular

routine of duty every day, and it was Miss Primula's boast that none of the family had ever been guilty of the least indecorum. That not even she had ever beheld Mr. Joshua in his shirt sleeves, and that she had never yet appeared before him in curl-papers and a wrapper. This was true.

Judge of Mr. Joshua's feelings, then, when one night he was awakened by a ringing of the door-bell, and hurrying down found one of his neighbors at the door, who begged his pardon, but told him that it had become necessary that he should see to his sister's welfare.

"And where is my sister?" gasped Mr. Joshua.

"On the back fence," replied the neighbor, as gravely as he could. And on the back fence Mr. Joshua found Miss Primula, evidently asleep, and in great danger, if she should awaken suddenly.

She was no longer young, nor had she had any practice in acrobatic performances; but there she was, in night-gown, ruffled cap and slippers, walking on the top of the fence as we sometimes see little boys do, balancing herself with her arms, and while the spectators, quite a party of whom had assembled, watched her with breathless interest, and did their best to protect her from injury, she made the tour of the two back gardens, and at last let herself down to the ground on a grapevine trellis, in quite a scientific manner. The jar of descent awoke her, suddenly, and the shock, as well as her intense mortification, made her quite ill for several days—especially as her brother was so deeply mortified that he could not restrain his reproaches, and said rather frequently:

"I would not have believed it of you, Primula, had an angel told it of you."

ABOVE THE WHIRLPOOL AT MIDNIGHT.

And now I remember another instance of the sort, told me by a guest of the hotel at Trenton Falls, N. Y., when I was there with Mr. Dallas upon our wedding trip.

If you have been to those falls, you know the narrow path upon the rocks above the whirlpool, guarded only by a little chain (when I saw it)—the place where once, upon a time, a bride in her honeymoon, dropping her expensive lace-trimmed handkerchief, stooped to catch it and fell.

For days her body was seen whirling about in that dreadful water, and the poor bridegroom watched it, moaning and weeping, refusing to leave the spot, though nothing that fell into that whirlpool was ever gotten out again, and he should never be able even to lay his young wife's body in the grave.

This story had one day been told, upon the very spot, to a guest, a sensitive lady, who was much affected by it. She became so nervous that it was with difficulty her husband got her safely to the hotel again, and she was obliged to retire at once. That night a frightful storm arose, and in its midst the gentleman awoke to find his wife gone. As she was a somnambulist, his terror was very great. He discovered that she was not in the hotel, and, procuring lanterns, they went out in search of her.

THE FREED SPIRIT.   53

The rocks near the whirlpool were so slippery with sleet that the men could scarcely keep their footing in rubber boots, but there was the lady, in night attire, bare-headed, quietly seated on the rocks. Fortunately, the men who discovered her obeyed her husband's orders and were quiet, and neither touched nor spoke to her, and finally she arose and came quietly forward.

The whirlpool was left behind when she awoke, but her terror was excessive, and, as usual, she had known nothing of her escapade, though the story of the drowned bride had haunted her before she went to sleep and made her most unhappy.

I believe that she did not suffer in any way from exposure to the cold, though her feet were bare and she wore nothing but fine white muslin.

The somnambulist never falls, or slips, or strikes his head, or bruises or strains himself, save when he is suddenly awakened. While asleep, he seems to lead a charmed life and to be much better able to take care of himself than in a normal condition.

CHAPTER 6.

DREAMS.

I know a lady, a farmer's wife, who always dreams of a red cow, before news of death reaches her, or before death enters the family.

I know another who always dreams of a little baby before calamity of any sort. She judges of what is to happen by the baby's conduct. If it is a sick child and weeps, death is about to deal a blow; if it smiles, the trouble is but transitory, and once, when a heavy and utterly unexpected pecuniary loss came upon her, a loss that utterly changed her life, she dreamed of the tiniest infant with the face of an old usurer, who carried in his hand a bag of money—a ludicrous fact enough, but still a fact.

The dreaming of prophetic dreams has not been given to me, though often I could think afterward that such and such a dream foreshadowed some event, usually a sad one.

I have had in that twilight of the senses, between the night of slumber and the day of perfect awakening, experiences that fully foretold sorrows close at hand: always sorrows, never joys—one of them too recent to write down here, in detail. I can only say that a face floated before me, and words were heard by me, which fully delineated an event which robbed my life of happiness, and the tidings of which were brought to me almost as the vision passed, and that when I had no reason to apprehend calamity, but was waiting for the return of the dear one in perfect security.

I have dreamed terrible dreams, which actually frightened me, but none of the incidents which occurred in them ever actually came to pass. Once, I remember, however, that I attended the reception of a bride. The presents were displayed in a room up-stairs, some of them on a marble-topped centre-table. That night I dreamed that I went to the same house and went up-stairs to the small room where I had looked at all those pretty gifts. As I entered, I saw a white rose lying on the bright-flowered Brussels carpet, and, stooping to pick it up, saw on the marble table, instead of the pretty trifles of silk and velvet that had covered it, a small coffin—then I awoke. But nothing happened to the bride or the groom. It was two years later, or nearly so, that I went to that house again to attend the funeral of a tiny infant. The person who stood at the door signified that I was to go up-stairs. I entered once more the little room I have spoken of, and the first thing that met my eye was a white rose lying on the gay carpet. It had fallen from the roses heaped upon the baby's coffin, which stood on the marble table, just as I had seen it in my dream.

But why should such a thing have been foretold to *me*? The house was the house of a person I liked, but was not particularly intimate with; the brief life was in no way linked with mine. I was sorry for the mother, that was all. It was one of the sad things of the world, but why should *I* have dreamed of it two years previously?

I know of several very singular dreams that surely "meant something," that did not come of the thoughts of the day.

Yet even those that do "show how we may be perceptive of that which is not and never may be, rendering it possible that we may be equally perceptive of that which shall be."

MY SISTER'S DREAM.

Amongst our most intimate friends were, and still are, the family of Mr. William B. Carlock. At the time of the story I am about to relate, there lived with them in their home a cousin of Mrs. Carlock's, named Caroline Grace, a very neat, mild, pleasant young lady, in somewhat delicate health, who was very nice to the children, and who had, I remember, the faculty of telling the exact time at any moment without reference to a watch or clock.

She could be awakened out of the soundest sleep to do this, and was always true to a second.

One morning my sister Julia, then a very little girl, not more than five years old, came down to breakfast, very anxious to tell a dream that she had had. She thought it very amusing. She had dreamed that Mrs. Carlock was "buttering" the sheets that lay upon a bed in her house and saying "oh, how hot, poor Caroline!"

We children thought it a "funny dream," and mother made a remark to the effect that it was singular to dream of such a particular housekeeper as Mrs. Carlock buttering the sheets of a bed.

No one thought seriously of the dream : we were in the habit of telling such dreams to each other as were comical—anything that would awaken a laugh. I believe most children are.

Nothing more was said about the dream that day, and by evening we had nearly forgotten it. We had gone out upon the door steps to look at something in the street, when we saw a woman coming toward us whom we knew to be often employed in Mrs. Carlock's family, as she had been in ours. She was a professional nurse, in fact, and was apt to arrive whenever the storks brought a new baby to either house.

I remember her big bonnet, her full-skirted woolen dress and her large plaid shawl, as if it were yesterday. She seemed very weary and very low-spirited, and she sat down upon the steps and asked us to tell mother and grandmamma that she would like to see them a moment. This we did, and they came at once. Then she burst out with the words :

"Oh, ladies, ladies! I've been at Mrs. Carlock's all day—Caroline Grace is burnt to death."

Of course, we were all horror-stricken, and she went on to tell us that Miss Grace had risen very early, before any one else was up, and gone down stairs. How she set herself on fire no one ever quite knew, but she was seen rushing about the garden in a light flame, all her garments blazing. In her agony and terror she fled from those who were trying to save her, into the house again, up stairs and down. At last Mr. Carlock caught her and enveloped her in a blanket, as he had been vainly endeavoring to do all the while. Her clothes were burnt off, and all that they could do was to pour oil upon her.

At the time my sister was dreaming—for she awakened from the dream to come to breakfast—Mrs. Carlock was pouring oil upon a sheet with which they had covered the poor girl, and, no doubt, uttering ejaculations of pity, and the flesh of the sufferer, which had been roasted, was appreciably hot.

Certainly the dream was a strange one. It was "veridical," if ever dream was; but why, since the child dreamed it, she was not aware that some one was burned—why she should only see Mrs. Carlock engaged in buttering bed-linen, I cannot imagine. In her dream the terrible tragedy was simply an amusing incident.

A few years after this my sister dreamed that she saw Mrs. Jerome Thompson, the first wife of the artist, overset a kettle on her foot, and cry out that she was scalded. Nothing more—just that. A few weeks afterward I saw Mrs. Thompson, and she told me that she had been laid up with a scalded foot.

"I thought I *must* have a copper tea-kettle," she said, "and I bought a beauty, and was *so* proud of it; now I hate it.

"I went into the kitchen to warm my feet, and my skirt caught in the spout of the kettle as I turned away, and over it went."

And then she told me how it scalded all the instep and kept her confined to the house for several weeks.

I do not know whether the dream was dreamed at the time of the occurrence or not; I never spoke of it to Mrs. Thompson.

My dear mother once told me of a dream which certainly was a singular one. She had retired in a very pleasant mood, and had not been conversing on any subject likely to occasion dismal dreams. Yet, in her sleep, she thought that she awakened, anxious and sorrowful, and that there was a sound in the room that she could not account for; then a movement, and she thought that she saw that the window was open, and that two black figures stood there, leaning slightly out, as if interested in something in the street. Then she clearly perceived that these figures were those of men, clad in black, and had stern and solemn faces. They held wound about their hands the ends of ropes, with which they seemed to be striving to draw something up from below.

With that quiet acceptance of astonishing things which is the peculiarity of dreams, she calmly inquired of the strangers—"who are you? and what are you doing there?"

One of the men turned his head and looked at her.

"We are drawing up the coffin," he said.

"Whose coffin?" she asked.

"That of Miss Betsy Palmer," he replied. At this instant she awoke, glad to find that she was only dreaming, and soon slept again.

The lady whose name had been mentioned was a dear friend, and one in whom my mother and grandmother took a great interest.

However, she had lately been heard of in perfect health, and there was no reason to feel any anxiety in regard to her safety. My mother attached no importance to the dream, and expected to hear shortly the usual interesting chat of daily pleasures or anxieties which Miss Palmer's correspondence always contained. But there were never to be any more of these pleasant letters. Shortly there arrived, from the old homestead in Long Island, one with the ominous black seal, that says so plainly, "I bring evil news." It was written by a stranger, I believe, and told that she was dead. A fever had broken out in the place; she had nursed several relatives, one a sister, and when this latter had breathed her last, Miss Betsy had simply said—"I am tired and must lie down." They found her dead.

A NEIGHBOR'S DREAM.

Once, upon a time, there lived in our neighborhood a brilliant politician, who, however, was not to be held up to the world as a perfect example of good morals.

Amongst other misdeeds, he staid out until the most unheard-of hours, and his wife had ceased to sit up for him, and regularly left him to his conscience and his latch-key.

One night the whole block was aroused by the ringing and rapping of a policeman at the politician's door. Word had been brought that he was drowned.

The poor woman was, naturally, in great grief, and to those who went to her in the hope of helping her, or, at least, of showing her their sympathy, she said that, when the policeman's knocks aroused her, she was dreaming that she saw her husband in a boat upon the water, in company with men and women, who wore upon their shoulders the heads of hideous beasts; that they leaped about in the boat, and all went over together.

The facts of the case were that he was in a boat filled with intoxicated men and women—brutes in human shape—for the time being at least, and that some of them, in a spirit of drunken fun, wildly rocked the boat from side to side and overset it.

The woman did not know that her husband was on the water, or anything whatever of his companions, and expected him to come home as usual when he felt inclined to do so.

THE PERSIAN RUG.

I knew a lady who was, one day, much pleased to receive, as a present, a very beautiful rug. She thought of it often, admired it immensely, and placed it in a conspicuous place in her parlor.

One night she dreamed of it—the dream was this:

Standing upon it, she looked down into a new-dug grave and saw her little boy, the pride of her heart, a healthy little creature, full of vitality and happy as the day was long, lying there, cold and dead.

She awoke with a shriek, and from that moment could not endure the sight of the handsome rug, of which she had previously thought so much. Of course, I should not tell this story here if that were all.

Three months later the child was taken ill and died.

The day of the funeral was wretched, the ground damp, the mother ill, but she would stay with the little one to the last.

After she was seated in the carriage, the person who supervised everything on the sad occasion, bethought him to get something that she might stand upon, and, going into the house, picked up this rug and had it taken to the place of interment.

Thus it came to pass that, as the mother looked down upon the child's coffin, she became aware of the rug beneath her feet.

It was as she had seen it, save that the coffin was now closed, and in her vision it was open. Crying out—"my dream has come true"—she fainted away in her husband's arms.

THE FINDING OF THE LAST CANTOS OF THE "DIVINA COMEDIA."

This is the story related by Boccaccio, of the finding of the last cantos of the "Divina Comedia" after the death of Dante:

"And those friends he left behind him, his sons and disciples, having searched at many times and for several months everything of his writing to see whether he had left any conclusion to his work, could find in no wise any of the remaining cantos; his friends generally being much mortified that God had not at least lent him so long to the world that he might have been able to complete the small remaining part of his work; and having sought so long and never found it, they remained in despair.

"Jacopo and Pietro were sons of Dante, and, each of them being rhymers, they were induced by the persuasions of their friends to endeavor to complete, as far as they were able, their father's work, in order that it should not remain imperfect; when to Jacopo, who was more eager about it than his brother, there appeared a wonderful vision, which not only induced him to abandon such presumptuous folly, but showed him where the thirteen cantos were which were wanting to the 'Divina Comedia,' and which they had not been able to find.

"A worthy man of Ravenna, whose name was Pier Giardino, and who had long been Dante's disciple, grave in his manner and worthy of credit, relates that, on the eighth month after his master's death, there came to his house, before dawn, Jacopo di Dante, who told him that that night, while he was asleep, his father, Dante, had appeared to him, clothed in the whitest garments, and his face resplendent with an extraordinary light; that he, Jacopo, asked him if he lived, and that Dante replied, 'yes, but in the true life, not our light.' Then he, Jacopo, asked him if he had completed his work before passing into the true life, and, if he had done so, what had become of that part which was missing, which none of them had been able to find. To this Dante seemed to answer, 'yes, I finished it,' and then took him, Jacopo, by the hand, and led him into that chamber in which he, Dante, had been accustomed to sleep when he lived in this life, and touching one of the walls, he said: 'what you have sought for so much, is here'; and, at these words, both Dante and sleep fled from Jacopo at once. For which reason, Jacopo said he could not rest without coming to explain what he had seen to Pier Giardino, in order that they should go together and search out the place thus pointed out to him—which he retained excellently in his memory—and to see whether this had been pointed out by a true spirit or a false delusion. For which purpose, although it was still far in the night, they set off together, and went to the house in which Dante resided at the time of his death.

"Having called up its present owner, he admitted them, and they went to the place thus pointed out; there they found a blind fixed to the wall, as they had always been used to see it in past days. They lifted it up gently, when they found a little window in the wall, never before seen by any of them, nor did they even know it was there. In it they found several writings, all moldy from the dampness of the walls, and, had they remained there longer, in a little while they would have crumbled away. Having thoroughly cleaned away the mold, they found them to be the thirteen cantos that had been wanting to complete the 'Comedia.'"

CHAPTER 7.

GHOST STORIES.

And now for a series of old-fashioned ghost stories.

I believe every one of them. The people who told them to me were in perfect earnest, and you can read them, if you feel inclined, and come to your own conclusions. About such things as these it is much better to write than to talk: it is much more satisfying to both parties. The reader can say—"now, what an idiot she must be to credit such a tale," or, to believe that she saw such and such a thing, without hurting the feelings of the writer; and the writer can prose on without any injury to the reader, who can close the volume and need not "beat his breast," as did the wedding guest who was detained by the ancient mariner to hear a frightful story, when he wanted to feast and dance, and be merry.

As intellectual food, ghost stories are "very filling." You can easily have a surfeit of them; but I am sworn to tell all I know this time—I do not believe I shall ever do it again.

I write them down for the motives I set forth in the first pages of this book, and for another. I want to convince *myself* if I can, that all these things are not phantasies of the brain, and I am firmer in my faith, I assure you, than I was when I wrote the first page.

Before the custom of making calls on New Year's day had quite come to an end in New York, we were directing envelopes for our cards, during Christmas week, when some one noticed that we had forgotten our friend, Mr. Blomgren. We hastened to correct our omission, and fell to speaking of Mr. Blomgren as one we liked particularly. He was amiable and unassuming, and had the most winning manners. In fact, he was a very fine specimen of the Swedish gentleman, and each of us had something pleasant to say of him, and we rejoiced that we had discovered our mistake in time for him to get his card, which we directed to his boarding place.

New Year's day came, and, during the afternoon, Mr. Blomgren did not present himself. However, we had rather thought that he would come in the evening and were not surprised.

It was about eight o'clock, I think, when one of us went up-stairs to put two little nieces, who were visiting us, to bed.

The children were sound asleep, and their aunt was growing drowsy, when she became aware of a tall figure standing in the door-way, and, starting up, saw that it was Mr. Blomgren, and fancied that, as the room was sometimes used as a dressing-room at our receptions, he had supposed that this would be the case to-night.

She arose and advanced toward him, saying words to the effect that every one was down stairs. He answered, without a smile—" I came because you sent me a card."

"We are delighted to see you, Mr. Blomgren," she

replied; "shall we go down?" But he was already gone, and she followed.

As he was not to be found in any of the lower rooms, and none of us had seen him, we decided that the mistake he had made had mortified him and that he had gone away at once, and we were all very sorry. Yet, it was not like him to be so sensitive, he was too much a man of the world, and not by any means a boy—thirty years of age, probably.

A few days after, a lady friend called, and one of us spoke of Mr. Blomgren. She had got so far as to say—"of course, we sent him cards"—when the visitor cried out:

"Sent him cards?—why, he had been dead a week or more on New Year's day."

He died of pneumonia, after a brief illness, and, having no relatives here, he was taken to a hospital.

I know that many people who knew him had no knowledge of his death until weeks after it occurred.

It is only fair to say that the lady who saw him afterwards decided that she must have been asleep and dreamed it all—though, she declared, it resembled no other dream that she had ever had, and she was not conscious of any waking.

A MISSISSIPPI PILOT'S STORY.

The authority for the following story is a sensible and honorable man, now nearly ninety years of age. Were I to give his name, many old western men would recognize it at once, for he was a well-known pilot of the Ohio and Mississippi steamers in their most important days. However, at the present time, he objects to being supposed to be a believer in the supernatural, and it would be a breach of faith to be more explicit. The tale, as it is told to me, is this:

In this gentleman's boyhood, he had the misfortune to lose a good and loving mother, and circumstances connected with his father's second marriage made his home unhappy. Consequently, he went to live with an uncle, where he did not find himself much happier. His material needs were never forgotten; but no one showed him any tenderness—he was very lonely and desolate, and this fact was noticed by the wife of a neighbor, who felt great pity for the motherless youth. She manifested this in various gentle ways, and the lad was very grateful. In time, pity and gratitude grew to be affection: the woman felt as if she had gained another son; the boy, as though he had found a second mother. Alas! when he was about fourteen years of age, death once more robbed him of his dearest friend and counselor. The warm-hearted woman died, to the great grief of all who knew her and loved her, but on none did the blow fall more heavily than on the poor boy, who felt himself once more alone in the world. The funeral took place upon one sad autumn day, and the boy, who had, of course, attended it, went home with a swelling heart, longing only to find some lonely place in which to weep. But no one understood his sorrow, and he was at once harshly ordered to go and feed the cattle. With a bitter feeling of loss and desolation upon him,

THE FREED SPIRIT.

he took his way through the twilight to the barn where the hay was stored.

The world looked as bleak and cold as though it knew the sun would never shine upon it again. All about him was gloomy: the withered grass, the bare branches, the old fences—no longer draped by the vines that covered them in summer—life seemed utterly without happiness, without friendship. Deeper and deeper grew his anguish; with heavy steps he reached the old barn door and entered, and, for awhile, indulged in the natural expression of his emotions, then set about his task, and, as he groped for the hay, he heard a soft, rustling sound for which he could not account, and, rising, with his arms full of hay, he looked toward the door. There, framed in the broad doorway, the fading light faintly illuminating her form, stood his kind, dead friend. No sheeted, shrouded figure, but apparently herself in her simple daily dress, looking well and happy.

A light, from whence he knew not, illuminated her face, and she gave him the cheery smile with which she always welcomed him during her lifetime.

There was nothing terrible in what he saw; but, nevertheless, knowing that his good friend was dead, the boy was overcome with terror, and escaping from the barn by another door, fled to the house. It was days before he recovered from the shock this kindly vision gave him.

I believe that if people were not encouraged to fear apparitions, we should know better what they mean, what they are.

Why, if they actually are the disembodied spirits of those who were good and true on earth, should they be things to flee from? We do not run from an old friend in a fresh dress.

Later, the boy wished that this terror had not fallen upon him, and that he had spoken to his loving friend, who could only have come in kindness. For years he believed that he had experienced a supernatural visitation; but, as he grew older, he came to consider it an hallucination, caused by his excited condition.

The events narrated in the second tale occurred years afterward, when the young man had fairly entered upon his career as a pilot, and had been married two years.

At that time the Ohio and Mississippi steamboats were the sole means of traffic and travel between the West and South. The journey to New Orleans was not, as it is now, a matter of a few days, but of several weeks. In the winter season, when ice blocked the upper portions of the stream, it was often much longer, and there was no medium of communication between the traveler and his home.

One day in early winter, the young pilot left Cincinnati for New Orleans, hoping that the rivers would remain open for some time, and fully expecting to meet his beloved wife and little child again in a few weeks. Both were well when he kissed them adieu.

The journey to New Orleans was made in an unusually brief time, and the return trip was without incident, until the mouth of the Ohio was reached, when it was found impossible to proceed further, on account of the ice with which the river was filled. Here the boat was detained several days, and, during that detention, the young pilot dreamed a dream.

He was at home again, but no one came to greet him. Wondering at this, he entered his door, and saw his wife lying in her coffin with her babe upon her bosom.

The dream was so terribly vivid that he could not rest. He left the boat and hastened across the country to the nearest point where mail communication with his home could be had, and here he found a letter conveying the terrible information that his wife and child were both dead. His dream was true.

He, however, takes a common-sense view of the matter, and believes that the dream was born of the anxiety of the detention and the longing to meet his dear ones once more.

DR. F'S STORY.

Dr. F., a well-known homœopathic physician of New York City, once gave me an excellent ghost story. The occurrence was fresh at the time, and he told it as two young ladies had just told it to him, only withholding their names.

The two girls lived with their mother in a flat, rather up town. Their bed-room was next to that the older lady occupied, and it was their custom to leave the communicating door open, that she might call them in case of need. A light usually burned in their mother's room, especially if she were not very well. This was the case one night, and one of the girls, waking suddenly, lifted herself on her elbow and looked toward the door. To her astonishment, she saw sitting beside her mother's bed, and looking at her intently, a lady in Quaker dress, wearing the borderless net cap that used to be the head-gear of a "female Friend," for the rest a gray dress and little shoulder-shawl. Fancying that her eyes deceived her, she touched her sister and whispered:

"Look, do you see anything in mother's room?" The sister instantly cried out: "Why, there is a Quaker lady there," and jumped out of bed. She saw the figure rise and glide toward the door; then it was gone. The mother was sound asleep,

The other girl, who had turned her face to the wall and shut her eyes, finally gained courage to rise and assist her sister in searching the room. The door, through which the figure had seemed to pass, was locked on the inside. There was no way by which any one could have entered. They knew that their mother's mother had been a Quakeress and always wore "the plain dress," and what they had heard of her appearance tallied with this that they had seen. They felt sure that their mother was about to die, and this really happened in a few days: an event which was not, however, surprising, as she had been in ill health for some time.

WHAT A MUSICIAN SAW.

A well-known musical composer is responsible for what comes next.

He was taking tea with some friends who had recently moved to a new house, aud his chair was placed at the table in such a way that he faced a door opening into a hall or passage.

While they were all talking, he saw a young man standing at the door, looking at them. He turned away in a moment; but the gentleman, who knew enough of the family to be sure that there was no such inmate of the house, yielded to an impulse that got the better of his decorum, sprang to his feet, looked out into the hall, and saw the young man pass through a door, which, if I am not mistaken, led down some cellar steps.

Returning to table, he apologized for his conduct, and was told that they guessed what he had seen, that they often saw it, and were no longer alarmed or startled when it presented itself.

My memory on the subject is accurate as to general facts, but not as to detail. I know that they saw this young man in the parlor, reading; in the garden, and all over the house; but whether they then knew of, or afterward saw, a photograph of a gentleman who formerly lived there, and which resembled this apparition, I do not remember.

At all events, as the tale ran, they did see one, and heard that its original died there very slowly and anxious to live. That he was peculiarly fond of the house, and that his invalid habits of lounging about, looking in at the doors, etc., etc., were those of this figure with which they all grew familiar and which their guest saw plainly enough to describe.

I believe in this case there was no vanishing: the

figure walked in and out just as a living person might, and finally ceased to appear at all.

It was generally supposed that a dislike to leave the world and an attraction for the house was the cause of this particular spirit's lingering. No tragedy was connected with his death, nor did he seem to come in an alarming fashion. He seemed so like a living person, that had there been any possibility of a deception being practised, those who saw him would have fancied that some one simply walked in and out to amuse himself.

That is the way I remember the story, and, at all events, I am sure of the good faith of the narrator.

THE GHOST IN THE BACK PARLOR.

Now, whenever I make myself the heroine of a story in this book, I am on honor not to "embellish," and to tell you, as far as I can, just what happened, without adding anything to make the story better, and I shall do it in this case.

I wish some good spiritualist could explain the *raison d'etre* of the apparition which appeared to me in the back parlor of our home one evening. For an apparition it was, though it had nothing to do with me, and it came when the surroundings were entirely commonplace.

Going down to dinner in a pleasant mood, with nothing on one's mind to cause serious thoughts, is not a "condition" to invite spectres. Six o'clock is not the hour for them, but that was the time this shade elected to appear.

It was winter, and the gas was lit in my room, and out of doors it was quite dark. When the dinner-bell rang, I naturally went down-stairs. Every one else was already in the dining-room. I was the last to descend. As I passed through the lower hall, I noticed that the servant had neglected to light either the hall or the parlors, and went into the door of the front room for the purpose of getting a match. I found the box, and took out one match after the other, but they all seemed to be damp or defective and went out as I scraped them on the under side of the mantel-piece. The rooms were arranged as city parlors usually are; the long front-room, the square back-room, both were utterly dark, the inside shutters were shut, the shades down, the curtains dropped. We had all been occupied elsewhere and the room remained as it had been when the house was closed the night before.

There was not a gleam of light anywhere; yet, at this moment, I was aware of something lighter than the darkness passing to and fro at the end of the back parlor. I might describe it as "something gray." When I first saw it, it was the height of a large girl or a short woman, and I thought it was one of my sisters, and said, calling her by name: "Won't you find a match for me; these will not light?" There was no answer. The figure now crossed the room again, seeming to be taller, and I said: "Who is that? Won't you find a match, there are plenty on the table?" Again there was no answer, and again the figure crossed the room, and was as tall as a very tall man.

"Oh," I said, thinking that I now knew who was there,

and that the person was trying to frighten me. "That is *you* there in the dark. Light the drop lamp, please."

The figure advanced toward the centre of the room, and a light began to glow. I saw a hand on a level with the globes of the chandelier; from the palm, as though a match were held, not by the thumb and finger, but between the second and third with the fingers stiff, shone a blue light. It grew larger and looked like an electric light. I saw the globes of the chandelier and below them I saw a head. Slowly I became aware of a man with black hair, black side-whiskers and wearing evening dress, save that he had no collar on, no tie, but *had* a gold collar-button at his throat. I remarked the brilliant blackness of the cloth, and the peculiar jetty hue of the hair and whiskers; but over the features, from forehead to chin, lay what looked like a wet and wrinkled piece of fine linen. I only saw the figure to the knees, where all ended in shadow.

At this point, horror possessed me; I shut my eyes and uttered a wild war-whoop, which brought everybody to the parlors at once. Search was made; no stranger could have been in the house, the family were all at table, the cook in the kitchen, the other girl busy in the dining-room.

I was laughed at, I laughed at myself and nothing came of my delusion or illusion. Certainly, it was no so-called "warning," no omen of ill to any of us, but I only utter the exact truth when I assure my reader that, a year later, as we were moving from the house, I mentioned what I called "the back-parlor ghost," to a neighbor, who said:

"But, of course, you knew that a man hung himself in that room some years ago."

I had not. At first I refused to believe the statement; but it appears to have been so, though I never heard anything more than the simple fact that he hung himself, fastening the rope to a hook in the ceiling.

A HAUNTED MAN.

What I am now about to write will strike many people as too absurd to be believed, and, yet, I assure them that it is positively true, if the serious statements of respectable and intelligent people, with no disposition whatever to joke about anything, and who bear some of the weight of the affliction, are not to be set aside as valueless.

It is, indeed, a very terrible story, and it has ruined one life and saddened others, and the end is not yet.

It is now many years ago since a young gentleman, whom we will call "Y," attended one of the circles for spiritual manifestations that were then so common in Boston. The usual things happened, the tables tipped, raps were heard and messages spelled out. The youth was deeply interested, and, going home, full of the new idea, began to tell all that he had seen to his relatives.

"I'll show you how they do it," he said, and gathered all the young people, nothing loth, about a table. There they sat, their hands spread out, their fingers touching, and nothing happened until the youngest— then but five years old—insisted on being taken into the circle. Then, indeed, the table began to tip, and, all being in serious earnest, it was certain that no voluntary movement was made by any of the party.

Not only did the table move, but raps were heard, and sounds like the falling of drops of water upon stone. I believe that words were spelled out that night, but certainly they were afterward, for the young people fell into the habit of forming circles every evening. Before long, they made at least one discovery—none of the phenomena occurred when the little child was absent; his presence in the circle was necessary. Not a rap came; not an inch did the table stir, unless he was present.

It was plain that he was the medium, and, before long, the most serious things occurred in his presence. China was flung from the pantry shelves, books thrown from the table, sounds were heard like the beat of rain, or the falling of a shower of sand, and blows fell on the ceiling and walls, as though an unseen carpenter were hard at work. The child now began to declare that he saw things that the others did not see—spoke of the man, or the woman, who came into the room, who met him on the stairs. Friends and neighbors began to drop in to enjoy the mysterious happenings. The father of the family, a busy man, who was not aware for a time how far his young people were going, grew alarmed and forbade them to hold any more circles in his house. The young people of the Y family were obliged to obey, but others had houses—the circles were held elsewhere. The little boy went about with his brothers and sisters, and the phenomena which occurred in his presence grew more important.

The being who appeared to be behind the scenes in these circles, gave itself a name, and was shortly spoken of as—so and so—just as one of the circle might have been.

It was continually promising to show itself, but declared that it could only do so in one place—the cellar of the residence which the Y family occupied—and it was resolved that, whenever the opportunity offered, this should be put to the test. Accordingly, when their parents were on one occasion obliged to leave home on business, the sons deliberately disobeyed their father, and invited the circle to meet again where it was originally formed.

The little medium—let us call him "Robbie"—being in their midst, all went swimmingly. Raps came in showers, and, being spelt out, commanded them to proceed to the cellar, make it perfectly dark, and watch until they saw him, for he would surely show himself.

It was all fun to the young people, and to the cellar they went, closed a shutter through which the moonlight streamed, ranged themselves in a row, extinguished a light which they had brought and waited for the promised manifestation.

The child stood between two of his brothers, who each held one of his hands, and, suddenly, he cried—"see—look—there"—and now, not only he, but every one else, saw at the end of the cellar a little white mist, that grew momentarily thicker and whiter and appeared to be forming itself into a ball. At last it began to gleam and glitter—something like the moon when it peeps from between the clouds on a misty night, or, as one of the beholders describes it, like broken quicksilver—and a little later began to shape itself into something like a monstrous face.

Just at this juncture, when all the beholders were growing nervous, little Robbie was suddenly lifted into the air and held in a horizontal position. He still clung to his brothers' hands, and screamed wildly to them to save him—but all their efforts were in vain: they could no more place him upon his feet or take him in their arms, than if some mighty giant had prevented them. The child appeared to be going into convulsions. The indescribable object at the end of the cellar looked more like a fiendish face than ever; confusion reigned, the lamp was overset, but at last some one managed to find the window and flung open the shutter. The evening light, faint as it was, seemed to banish whatever it may have been that they looked upon. Little Robbie's feet came to the ground; he clung sobbing to his older brother, who gathered him to his bosom and carried him up-stairs, and the thoroughly terrified party of young people dispersed to their separate homes.

Little Robbie was very ill for weeks. The truth had to be told to the parents, and no more circles were held. In fact, they could not be, for the child could not now have been persuaded to take his place in one.

However, from this time, he was for years followed by raps and strange sounds of all sorts. Glass would seem to be broken near him, stones to fall, feet to patter—some unseen thing followed him about the house, and all the family, and every guest in the house, heard the sounds. Above all, the doors and windows of the room he occupied were opened continually by unseen hands.

I forgot whether this state of things came to an end suddenly or slowly; but, at all events, I believe that he was entirely delivered from the affliction by the time he was twelve years old. He attended school like other boys, he went to college, he studied medicine and began to practice.

The very memory of those days when he was tormented, as we have described, was hateful to him. Had there not been so many witnesses to the phenomena, he might have been able to believe them all the result of some disorder of the brain; but several sane and sensible people attested to all that had occurred, and all that he could do was to strive to forget the past.

At last he married, and his life went on like that of other happy men for some years. Suddenly, however, a great woe befell him: his wife died. He grieved bitterly, but in time found solace in his profession, and passed most of his leisure in reading. He had been a widower, I think, about two years, when, one day, as he sat in his own room, reading something that demanded close attention, he was considerably annoyed by a pattering sound. It was as though a shower of gravel was falling close beside him. He looked up, but saw nothing. However, resuming his reading, the noise began again, with other sounds of a like nature, and with a horror passing all words, he understood that the affliction of his childhood was again upon him; and this, indeed, was so. Only the demonstrations were even more powerful and unpleasant. At first they occurred only in his own home; but soon they followed him to the houses of his patients, where noises, the origin of which could not be traced to any ordinary agency, occurred in the rooms of invalids, whose lives depended on perfect quiet. Chairs were overturned, tables jerked violently. A sofa, on which a sick man lay, was dragged into the centre of the room, as if by invisible hands.

When the poor doctor, in despair, confessed that these manifestations were in some way caused by his presence—were the work of his familiar or attendant demon—those who could not deny that they occurred were afraid of him, and others thought him mad. He was obliged to give up his practice and take up his abode with friends, as one afflicted with some terrible disease might, hoping that time would effect a cure.

But nothing of the kind has happened. On the contrary, it is positively averred by those who live in the house with him that the noises follow him continually, and that, night after night, a sound like the beating of heavy sticks is kept up upon the headboard of his bed, or the walls of his room—a sound audible everywhere in the house. Heavy footsteps are heard on the floor, locked doors are opened—if there is a season of quiet at times, the disturbance is only the greater when it is renewed. And the man on whom this strange trouble has fallen—driven from the ranks of his profession, overwhelmed with grief and shame—is dying of it, dying slowly and in agonies of horror.

Delicacy forbids me to use the name of the family in this instance; but it is one well known and much respected, and in no way does the gentleman, who seems to be pursued by a veritable fiend, seem to have merited the persecution—which fell at first upon an innocent child and has continued through the years of an industrious and sober manhood.

CHAPTER 8.

A COVINGTON APPARITION.

A young man, who lived at the time in Covington, Ky., was standing at the door of his house one evening, when a lady in very deep mourning, with her veil over her face, came up the steps and inquired if his mother were at home.

He said that she was, opened the parlor door and asked her to be seated. Then, closing the door again, he went out upon the steps, speaking to some one who went to call his mother, and never being, for one moment, out of sight of the door of the parlor, which remained closed. Beside this, there was some one else on the door-step at the time.

In a few moments his mother came down stairs and went into her parlor—instantly calling out, "why did you send for me? there is no one here." And there was not.

The parlor was a long one, occupying the whole of that side of the house. There was no other door in it but that by which the lady in black had entered. The windows remained closed, so that the idea that some one had taken pains to play a trick and climb out of them was untenable. No one could have passed the young man on the front door-step, and he not only saw the figure, remarked the depth of its mourning, and the solemnity of its demeanor, but heard it speak and replied to it, and saw it seat itself as an ordinary caller might.

A REPROACHFUL GHOST.

A story vouched for by Mr. A.

In common with many other men in New York City, Mr. A, who had lost his position in some public office, and consequently was anxious concerning the welfare of his family, was making every effort to find another.

He had a wife and several children dependent upon him, and had no savings, and he naturally left no stone unturned in his efforts to place himself. He went everywhere where such abilities as he possessed were needed, wrote to every one who had any influence, and, finally, remembering that Mr. B—a friend whom he had obliged and who had promised to do anything in his power for him—employed several gentlemen in his office, went to him.

Having stated his case, the friend ejaculated, "Why didn't you come to me a month ago? I had exactly the place for you; but I had no idea you wanted one, and gave it to young X, who was overjoyed to get it. He wants to marry, and this is the first good thing he has had."

"And I am married and have a houseful of children," said the other, despondently.

"Well, if I had had a hint from you, you should have had the place," said B; "no one else could have come before you. To be sure, I haven't pledged myself to

X ; I could dismiss him at once, but he will feel it very much."

"Well, he is a young man and has a mother's home to live in," said A; "I would not try to oust another man, of course, but I'm at my last cent—I may be set into the street for all I know. A single man can do many things a married man cannot."

"I'll think it over, my dear fellow," said B; "of course, my heart is with you, and if X gives me any excuse for telling him that he is not the right man in the right place, I promise you that you shall hear from me at once."

A then took his leave, feeling uncertain as to the result, and sincerely hoping that X would give B the excuse he desired for dismissing him.

On Saturday night he had heard nothing; the new month began on Monday, and on Sunday night he retired to bed, disconsolate.

The family were sound asleep and the house closed. It was a nice flat, and the outer door was fastened, of course, as well as the door below. Therefore, when the wife was awakened by a knocking at the bedroom door, she was much astonished.

Listening for a moment, she decided that she had been mistaken and composed herself to sleep again; but the knocking was repeated and was louder than before, and she touched her husband on the arm. Some one was certainly knocking at the inner door, which opened from the little private passage, though they knew that the door at the end of this had been fastened when they went to bed.

Filled with astonishment, Mr. A arose, put on a dressing-gown and slippers, and, going to the door, opened it cautiously. A lamp always burnt in the passage all night, and by its light he saw the figure of a man standing before him. It advanced, and he saw that it was young X, pale as death, who fixed upon his face dull and despairing eyes, and said:

"B will give you that place on Monday"—then was no longer there.

A ran to the door—it was fastened; he opened it and went down stairs; he searched the rooms and found nobody there. At last, trembling with excitement, he returned to bed, and told his wife that X had come to tell him that B would give him his place on Monday, and that he looked as if his heart were broken.

"At this time of night! why, how could he get to our door?" Mrs. A asked.

That Mr. A could not explain, nor how X had got out of the passage, nor why he should come at all. Then he descanted on the paleness of the young man's face, the strangeness of his departure, and Mrs. A said, "my dear, you've evidently been dreaming." "But you heard the knock—you aroused me to open the door," A replied. Mrs. A, much troubled about her husband, fearful that his anxiety had unsettled his mind, coaxed him to stop talking and go to sleep, which he finally did.

On Monday morning, as they were at breakfast, some one came in, a relative of Mrs. A's, who lived not far away. After the usual greetings, he said:

"We had a tragedy in our street last night, a young

man, who lives next door to us, shot himself—by the way, you know him, it was young X. He was engaged to a very pretty girl and has a mother who adored him. It will kill her, I think." Then he told this story:

A month before, after no end of ill luck, young X secured a fine position in B's place, and had been in splendid spirits. His wedding day was set, and the mother, who happened to like her prospective daughter-in-law, was arranging the house for the reception of the bride. She fancied that X would come home in a particularly pleasant mood on Saturday, for that happened to be the day on which he drew his first month's salary.

As soon as she saw him enter the door, she knew that some unpleasant thing had happened. He kissed her and sat down for a moment, took some money from his pocket and asked her to put it away.

"You are not ill, are you, my dear?" she asked, and he said: "No; but it wouldn't matter if I were, I'm no good to myself or any one else. I've lost my place, mother."

He was very gloomy that evening and throughout Sunday. His mother tried to cheer him and encouraged him to hope that he would find as good a position very shortly. She fancied that he retired in a happier mood, and, before leaving her, he kissed her very fondly many times. But that night he shot himself through the head, and was dead before the poor mother could procure assistance and open the door that he had locked on the inside.

Just as the caller reached this point of his tale, the postman's whistle was heard, and Mrs. A. went to the box and brought up a letter, which simply said: "The place is vacant; come on Monday.

B——"

For a moment A felt that nothing could make him take the position. But his wife and children sat before him, and there was no other prospect; he was, at the time the story was told to me, in B's office.

As for poor, young X, he lies in his early grave, his betrothed wife mourning him as young love mourns, and his old mother's heart is broken.

A SORROWFUL GHOST.

I am indebted for the following story to my friend, Miss ——.

About ten years ago, Mrs. B, of New Jersey, having been left a widow, found herself with an income insufficient for the support of her children. Consulting with her friends, they advised her to try taking boarders, and assisted her to secure a large boarding-house, whose proprietor was about to retire from business.

It was a handsome house and already full of boarders. Mrs. B had fine business talent and a charming manner, became a great favorite and prospered exceedingly.

When she took possession of the house, but one room was empty, a large, elegant and well-furnished apartment on the second floor. For this she soon found an occupant, who was at first delighted with it, but shortly became dissatisfied. What he did not like, he could not say; but if Mrs. B would put him in any other room in the house, he would be truly grateful.

A young couple, whose room was far less desirable, gladly made the exchange, and they in their turn soon begged to be placed elsewhere, and could give no reason.

Several other people tried the room, were delighted with it at first, and soon followed suit by begging to be placed anywhere else, and finally Mrs. B offered the discontented one the room she had given to her three boys, and gave the urchins this large and beautiful apartment. "Wasted it on them," as she said, laughingly, for it was really the best room in the house, and very attractive to strangers.

Two of the children were very small; the oldest was a boy of fourteen. For a time they seemed to enjoy their new quarters, but finally the youngest began to complain that he disliked the room. He did it so often and with so much energy, that his mother finally questioned him closely.

"Why don't you like that pretty room, darling?" she asked.

"I do' no," the child replied. He was yet too young to express his ideas. "I don't yike it."

"But why?" she persisted.

"I don't seep nice," he answered, whimpering. "He wakes me up evly time."

"Who does, your brother?" the mother asked.

"I do' no," the child replied again. "I don't want to seep in dat room."

Mrs. B made some change in the arrangements of the beds and heard no more complaints for several days; but, at last, in the middle of one quiet night, Mrs. B and her daughter were suddenly awakened by a tumultuous rapping upon her door and the voice of the oldest boy, crying: "Let us in, ma; let us in!"

Mrs. B opened the door at once, and in rushed the three boys, all pale with terror, the youngest clinging to the oldest brother.

"Well, now, children, what does this mean?" asked the aggravated matron. The oldest boy gazed reproachfully at her and said:

"We can't sleep, that is what it means. We haven't slept since we went into that room. If I tell you *why*, you'll think I want to frighten you, or else that I'm crazy."

"Well, I will tell, ma," said the second boy. "There's a fellow there."

"A fellow?" asked the mother.

"Yes," said the little boy. "He goes all around in the dark, and he shakes things and rattles things, and we tried to catch him, but we can't. He is there, for we hear him, but we can't see him."

"What folly!" said the mother. "No one could come into your room. Don't you lock your door?"

"He comes, and locking does not keep him out," said the boy. "And we are going to give that fellow the room to himself; we can't stand him."

"What fanciful children," said the mother.

"It's not fancy, ma," said the oldest boy. "It's just as brother says."

"Ess;" cried the baby, "he fwightens me. I don't yike dat room."

The children were disposed of elsewhere, charged to say nothing of their experience, and the objectionable room, after being carefully arranged, was locked up and left to itself.

Mrs. B considered her boarders whimsical, laughed at her boys for their folly, and naturally kept the story to herself. A ghost is not popular in a boarding-house, and the fancy that some living person could gain access to the sleeping apartments at midnight would be even less so.

It was a sunshiny summer afternoon when Miss Anna H——, a girl in her teens—arrived at Mrs. B's house to pay a visit of a few days. She knew nothing of the experience of the children, nor of the curious dislike that the boarders had exhibited for the handsomest room in the house.

She was in excellent health, never nervous, and of a cheerful disposition. The whole family inherit from their mother solid common-sense and admirably strong minds. They are very brave women, and not in the least superstitious, and are inclined to investigate whatever seems remarkable. Even at that early age, Miss Anna was not a girl to be frightened by odd noises, or "something white in the corner."

There was no talk of the room until bedtime, when Mrs. B said that she was glad to have one of the pleasantest apartments vacant, ushered Miss Anna upstairs, kissed her good night, and left her alone.

On this night the young lady was sleepy and tired, and having locked her door and said her prayers, hastened to bed and found herself almost at once in slumberland. She was an unusually sound sleeper, and it was not common for her to open her eyes until morning. However, that night, to her great surprise, she continually started awake, and always fancied that the cause was some curious noise directly in the room.

However, there was nothing there to make one, and finally, as day broke, the disturbance ceased and she slept soundly as usual.

She said nothing of her restlessness, passed a pleasant day and evening, and retired to her room at eleven o'clock.

She had not slept more than half an hour, when the apparent presence of some one in the room aroused her. She had fastened her door and knew that there could be no one there; but having passed one wakeful night, she was annoyed at the thought of enduring another, and wondered what it was that produced so singular an effect, for the sound was like some one moving cautiously about. The room was dark, and the young lady felt that it was best to remain where she was; but sleep having been completely driven away, she sat up in bed and listened intently.

Just then the town clock struck twelve—the proper hour for spectres—and the sound of some one sighing, sobbing, lamenting under his breath, came to her ear.

The slats of the blind shutters began to move slowly, opening and shutting at regular intervals, as they do when they are fingered by people who are peeping out, and a rocking-chair near the window began to sway slowly to and fro, with a creak for every motion. The effect produced was that of a man rocking and bemoaning himself. It was not a woman's voice, but that of a man perfectly overwhelmed with sorrow.

No form was visible, not so much as a shadow. When the slat was opened, the lights in the street made every object dimly visible. After rocking and sobbing for awhile, the unseen form seemed to leave the chair and began to pace the room, touching the foot-board as he passed and still lamenting. Again he sat in the chair. The bed shook violently when the unseen spectre touched it, and Miss Anna dreamed nothing of this, for she remained sitting up, broad awake, until daylight, watching and noting every sound from the striking of the midnight hour.

As day broke, the chair stopped rocking, the shutter slats ceased to move, the feet no longer trod the floor, nor were there any more sighs or sobs or lamentations.

Miss Anna, feeling assured of this, breathed a weary sigh and endeavored to compose herself to sleep, but in vain. She was not frightened, but felt as one who had been obliged for hours to contemplate the utter misery of another, without being able to alleviate it. She was simply worn out, and resolved on no account to spend another night in that room.

At the proper time that morning, she told her hostess of her resolution to shorten her visit, and, since it was necessary to excuse herself, told the tale.

On this, Mrs. B, after an attempt to laugh at the "ghostly visitation," confided to Miss Anna the previous history of the room and the tale her boys had told. During the conversation, a caller was ushered in.

She was an old resident of the place and one who had formerly boarded in that house.

In her excitement, Mrs. B lost her reticence, and told the story over again to her friend, who, after hearing the narrative, said:

"I suppose you know that poor young Mr. J occupied that room?"

"Who was young Mr. J?" asked Mrs. B. "I never heard of him."

"He was a very fine young man, who boarded here," the lady answered. "The girl to whom he was engaged died suddenly, about Christmas time. All the night before Christmas he was heard moving about his room, sighing and weeping, and as day broke on Christmas morning, he left the house, went to the D. graveyard, and there shot himself."

POOR HANNAH PENNY.

In a small town in Long Island, there lived at one time a gentleman, who, though he had a wife and several children, was not blind to the charms of a pretty servant maid named Hannah Penny. Particulars are superfluous, suffice it to say that the poor girl one day hung herself, leaving a letter which explained why life had grown to be too heavy a burden for her.

The gentleman's wife and children were in New York at the time, and at first the injured wife thought that nothing could induce her to forgive her husband. However, a good woman will not readily separate herself from the father of her children.

The sinner was penitent, poor Hannah was in her grave, and finally the lady returned to her home. The little ones were told that Hannah was dead, but knew no more.

The house was a large one, with a fine garret, where the children always played on rainy days, and thither they went as usual one stormy morning. When they came down to dinner, one of them, a little girl, said to her mother—"that wasn't true about Hannah Penny being dead, was it?"

The mother managed to falter: "Yes, dear; Hannah is certainly dead—do not talk of her."

But the younger girl called out:

"Oh—she isn't dead, mamma; truly, she isn't; she has been playing with us all the morning." The little boy added his word—"oh, yes; she came out of the long wardrobe and she played, only she wouldn't talk."

"Not a word," said his sister; "only shook her head and smiled." The other girl corroborated this statement, and said: "I suppose she has a cold and is too hoarse."

The children then added that after a while she went into the wardrobe again.

There was no stopping their little tongues; a new servant, who was in the room, repeated the story. My informant lived in the neighborhood at the time, and was aware of the excitement it caused in the neighborhood, and knew also that the innocent little ones constantly declared that, whenever they went to the garret, Hannah Penny came out of the wardrobe. She did not always play—sometimes she only looked at them.

The servants questioned them constantly, and they could describe her dress and tell how her hair was arranged, and the statements coincided accurately.

Hannah had been their nursery maid, and they were fond of her, and though she seemed to have grown dumb, were delighted to have her again after having mourned her as lost; but their innocent prattle aroused so much curiosity and so revived the tale of sin and horror, that neither the guilty man nor his injured wife could endure it. They left the place for ever and the house was sold to strangers, who occupied it in peace, seeing nothing of poor Hannah Penny, who had never appeared as an avenging spirit, but only with loving smiles and gentle glances for the innocent little children who had always loved her and with whom she had frolicked as though she had been a child herself. Indeed, she was little more in years, though she had had a woman's sad experience.

THE TWINS.

An officer of the Seventy-first Regiment, during war time, and now a very practical business man, told me that in his childhood he had had a most curious experience.

He had little twin brothers, with whom he was very fond of playing. He used to sit on the floor with them and throw pillows at them, and they, as well as they could, at him. He used to have all sorts of romps, in which pillows played a part, with the little ones, and they were very happy together.

But, alas!—one day one of the twins fell ill, and in a short time died. The remaining twin was unhappy without him. The larger boy grieved deeply and for some time romps were suspended. However, at last, the two children began their games again, and one day the little boy had just rolled the baby over on the pillow, while it crowed with glee, when he saw standing, close beside it, the other twin, exactly as he was in life, as solid and palpable to all appearances as his brother; but as the elder child sprang toward it, it vanished.

A servant—an old nurse, I believe—interpreted this vision to mean that the child had "come for its brother," and in two weeks the little creature was also "on the other side."

A PRETTY STORY OF HELEN HUNT JACKSON.

According to *a pretty story*, there is a poor woman in a Western State, who believes that she has seen the spirit of Mrs. Helen Hunt Jackson, the well-known authoress.

She was one of this lady's many protégés, though she had never seen her. Mrs. Jackson had been told that the poor woman was in need of clothing for a new-born babe, and, though unable to leave her room, had the garments her own little one had once worn collected and sent to her, with such a gentle message as one mother might send to another in such an hour.

Before the recipient of this kindness was able to call on Mrs. Jackson, in order to thank her in person, that lady died.

Not long after, the poor woman, having just bathed and dressed her child, was holding it up before her and admiring it, as mothers do, when suddenly a warm impulse of gratitude filled her heart, and she said aloud:

"Oh, baby, if only the dear, good lady that gave you those pretty clothes could see you now!" and was aware of a presence near her, and, looking up, saw, as she said, the loveliest lady she ever looked upon, standing near her. The stranger smiled and was gone. No living person had entered the room, she was assured, and she was certain in her own mind that she had seen the spirit of her benefactress.

Those who knew Mrs. Jackson say that she drew a perfect picture of her as she was in life, in describing the face and figure that she had looked upon.

CHAPTER 9.

NURSE KIRKPATRICK'S STORIES.

Nurse Kirkpatrick died long ago. Besides, were she living, she would be very proud of being "put into a book," and would have no objection to proclaiming her experiences from the house-top.

She was an elderly woman, who always appeared at our house at the same time that a new baby arrived there—and, as it was the general opinion of the wee-folk of the family that the angels had entrusted the new-comer to her care, and that she brought it in her large traveling-basket, she was regarded by us with awe and admiration.

She was, as her name indicates, Irish by birth, and very fond of talking, and scarcely ever did she enter the kitchen to make catnip-tea for the baby, or concoct gruel or panada, without telling some marvelous story.

As I was always at her heels, I heard everything, and I wish I could remember all I listened to.

Since those old French romances—"Cinderella"—"Prince Sincere"—"Riquet with the Tuft"—"Puss in Boots"—"Graciosa and Percinet"—you know the set, old as our great-grandmothers—were written and translated, no one has given children a real fairy-tale.

Those who have attempted to cater to the universal longing of all generations, have been so deeply impressed with the fact that they were writing nonsense, that they have either felt obliged to make their stories allegorical, to wind up with a moral, or, in some other cruel way, to disappoint the little readers, who want the bad fairy and the good—the pumpkin that turns into a chariot, the invisible cap, the purse of Fortunatus, the seven league boots, the ring that had but to be rubbed to bring superhuman aid to its possessor—and all the other occult mysteries which they accept without a question.

A fairy story, told by one who believes it solemnly, is, therefore, a delightful thing to listen to—and this Irish woman had no more doubt as to the truth of her tales of fairy-wells and fairy-rings—of the little fairy-cobbler, who prays the shoemaker to help him mend the slipper of the fairy-queen, and, if the act of kindness is done readily, rewards the cobbler with more money than he ever saw before in all his life; of the fairy-baker who has broken his peel and makes the amiable person who cuts him a new one, a rich man for life; of the girl who goes to peep at the good-people dancing at midnight, and is carried away into the hills, whence she returns, still young and blooming, when her school-mates are old men and women; of the changeling, deformed and miserable, left in the cradle of the smiling pet of the household, who has been spirited away to Elfin-land, than of her own existence.

That story about George Washington and his little hatchet never appeared so profoundly true to me as did these narratives.

But Mrs. Kirkpatrick told other things, that made

black Sally Ann, as she declared, "turn all gooseflesh," as she listened.

That of Beesy's sweetheart was very touching.

Beesy was Mrs. Kirkpatrick's intimate friend, when she was a young girl, still "living on the ould sod," and Beesy had a sweetheart named Johnnie, and he, like Jamie in the ballad of "auld Robin Grey"—"saving a croon piece, had naething left beside"—and "to make the croon a pound," made up his mind to seek his fortune in America.

"And at that time," Mrs. Kirkpatrick declared, "they thought goold was to be had in New York for the stooping to pick it up out of the strates."

With hopes akin to this, Johnnie kissed his Beesy, halved a broken sixpence with her, and went away, promising to come back "the minute he was rich, and marry her that day."

And, after awhile, one letter came, saying that he "had an illigant place," and Beesy was happy for awhile, and sent her answer and waited for more news from Johnnie. But none came, and Beesy grew pale and thin and spent her nights in tears, and at last confided to her friend that she feared Johnnie was false to her.

One evening, work being over, the two girls walked out together after dark—and Beesy grew quite desperate, and Maggie was trying to comfort her, pacing up and down a long hedgerow—with only the stars overhead, and all as still as if they were alone in the world, and neither able to see the other's face; but at last, the moon began to rise—a full-moon, big and yellow, and one side of the hedge was flooded with light, so that every leaf and every thorn was visible. And, all in a moment, Maggie saw Johnnie standing there, close up against the dark foliage.

He wore the gray clothes she had last seen him in, but no hat upon his head—and there was a yearning look in his eyes, and his arms were stretched toward his sweetheart.

"Now, glory be to God!—there's Johnnie himself come back and waiting to suprise ye!" cried Maggie—and Beesy turned and saw him and screamed out—"oh, my Johnnie! my darling Johnnie! do I live to see you again!" and rushed to cast herself into her lover's arms. But alas! no fond kisses, no warm embraces were to be hers—her hand only clasped the dark leaves of the moonlit hedge, while its thorns wounded her bosom—Johnnie was no longer there.

Then the poor girl cast herself upon the sod, and burst out wailing and weeping, crying that Johnnie was surely dead and that it was his wraith that they had seen. But Maggie would not believe it, and went running about, calling to Johnnie to show himself and to come to Beesy before she died of fright—berating him for playing such a joke.

"For it was like no ghost," she used to say, "but for all the world Johnnie himself, with his gray clothes upon him and his pipe sticking out of his pocket."

However, all the calling and crying produced no result, and at last Beesy was induced to go home—where Maggie felt sure she would find Johnnie waiting for her.

Sad to tell, this was not so, and a little later there

came a letter to Beesy from one of the "Sister" nurses in a hospital, to tell her that Johnnie was no more. He had sent his love, and the other half of the sixpence, and the few little things that he possessed, to Beesy, and spoke of her at the last.

"And sure it was Johnnie stood in the hedge that night," said nurse Kirkpatrick, "and no man else. I knew him too well to make a mistake in him."

Another of Mrs. Kirkpatrick's stories was more recent. It was about some one she called little Willie. He was the child of the people who lived in the house next door to the one she occupied.

He was a winning baby, just able to walk, and she was very fond of him, and often had him brought in to her. Indeed, small as he was, he could manage to get to the house himself—crawling down one set of door-steps and up the other with amusing dexterity, and bumping against the door-panels until he was admitted.

One evening she had been away from home for a week or so, and on her return was greeted by the news that little Willie had been very sick. She was very sorry to hear this and inquired particulars. The woman who lived down stairs was quite ready to give them, and stood leaning on the balustrades as she talked, while Mrs. Kirkpatrick, being weary, sat down on the lower steps of the stairs to listen.

She had just said, that as soon as she had taken something to eat, she would go in and see the child, when she beheld him enter the passage—not coming in at the door, but, as she said, "through the wall." He was in his night-gown and his feet were bare.

Petrified with astonishment, she could neither move nor speak, and before she could regain her voice, the other woman turned and saw the child.

"Bless us!" she cried. "Why, here is Willie—and with no shoes on his feet. What ails the woman to let him get away, and him just past the croup."

She stooped to take the child in her arms, but he was no longer there, and the hands of those who came to tell the news of his death were beating on the door.

* * * * * *

Strange to say, these stories never frightened, but only interested me, and I never doubted any of them.

HOW A SPIRIT SAT FOR ITS PHOTOGRAPH.

Once, upon a time, a gentleman who lived in St. Louis was happy enough to have a good and beautiful wife, whom he loved fondly.

However, while she was yet a young woman, she died, and he was left desolate.

After his first grief was a little softened, he began to regret very bitterly that he had no portrait of her. The fine picture by some famous artist, which they had decided to have painted in Paris, would now never exist, and his lost wife had always refused to sit for her photograph.

The poorest representation of her features would have been valuable to him now, and he blamed himself for not having urged her to have one taken.

One night, when he had fallen asleep thinking of this matter, he dreamed that a hand touched his, that he opened his eyes and saw his wife sitting beside him, dressed in a very beautiful white lace dress, which he greatly admired. She smiled and leaned across the pillow to kiss him:

"I should have done what you asked, my dear," she said. "I am sorry now, because you fret over it; but I have done what I could to please you. You will find my photograph in New Orleans; I sat for it to-day—I wore this dress."

She kissed him again and he awoke.

He was much agitated and moved to the point of shedding tears; but as he knew that his wife had not visited New Orleans since her childhood, though she was born there, merely supposed that the dream was the natural result of his thoughts. However, a few weeks later, he dreamed the same thing again, and this time heard his wife mention the street in which he would find her portrait.

"I have been trying in vain to make you dream of me, for nights," she said. And he thought he answered: "But I do dream of you very often." "Yes, in the dreams of sleep," she replied. "But this is a vision, a dream of the soul. It is I, myself, who tell you to go and get my picture, which you will find in —— street, in the city of New Orleans."

Again he awoke, this time much impressed; but as he believed that he knew that there was no portrait of his wife in existence, had no thought of going to New Orleans, or anywhere else, to find one.

Time passed on—his wife had been dead more than two years—when again he dreamed the same dream. This time he was awake, or believed himself to be so, and he took his wife's hands and held them.

"Dearest, I shall not come again," she whispered. "You will come to me one day, but never shall I return to you. If you want my portrait, you will find it where I have told you that it is." This time the hands seemed to melt in his; he saw the figure fade and believed that his wife's spirit had visited him. The next day he was on his way to New Orleans, and, on arriving, turned his steps toward the street mentioned. As he walked slowly along, a photographer's show-case caught his eye, and from it his wife smiled upon him in all the beauty of her prime. There could be no mistaking the fact. Besides, she wore the white evening-dress he knew so well, trimmed with lace of a peculiar pattern, and on her throat a necklace which he had had made to order for her.

He stood gazing upon it for a long while; then hastened up-stairs and questioned the photographer. The result was that in a little while they were exchanging confidences.

The widower had told his dream; the photographer had narrated his experience—it was this:

Some time before, he had fallen asleep in his studio, and had awakened to find that a lady had posed herself for a sitting.

She was dressed in white, and as if for the evening; but he fancied that she had left her wraps in the dressing-room.

Starting to his feet, he apologized, and felt that a conversation must have ensued; for, afterward, he remembered the size desired, and that the lady had said that her husband would come for the pictures; but he was sure that he must have been curiously confused, for he never could think just how all this was said, and sometimes fancied that not a word was spoken.

Also, he was unable to say when the lady left the studio. He waited for some time for her to return from the dressing-room, and was surprised when the young woman in attendance declared that no lady dressed in white had been there that day.

However, he finished the pictures, had a crayon head made and framed, and, coming to the conclusion that the lady who posed so well was an actress, took special pains that the work should be perfect. At last, however, he decided that all this had been in vain; that no one would ever come for the pictures, and placed the large crayon portrait in his show-case.

The picture had been taken about a year before. The lady had been dead more than two years, and had never been in New Orleans since she was five years old; but the husband not only paid for the photographs and the crayon head, but subsequently sent the photographer a check for a large amount.

Not half the value, he declared, of his inestimable treasure. People have tried to explain this story in several ways, but those most interested have always believed that, for once, at least, a spirit returned to earth to sit for its portrait.

* * * * * *

Another photographer, having taken a portrait of a baby, whose mother died at its birth, found behind the little bald head the face of a young woman, which was declared by those who had known her to be a perfect likeness of the child's mother.

He was greatly excited and deeply interested at the time, for he was sure that the plate was entirely clean and new. But, though he made many experiments afterward, he never had any other experience of the same sort.

THE STORY OF A WATCH.

The German family, who declare that this story is true, told it to one, who told it to me, twenty years ago.

The watch was then in their possession, and was a heavy, old-fashioned object, in a curiously engraved, double gold case. It had then recently been brought from Frankfort, and was worn by the oldest son of the gentleman of whom the incidents below are related.

This person, a physician of high standing and benevolent disposition, having discovered, in the poorest quarter of the town, an aged and well-educated old man, suffering from a disease that was inevitably mortal, caused him to be brought to his home, and there had him nursed and cared for as though he had been his own father.

The invalid was very grateful, and before he died, said to the physician: "When I am gone, I want you to keep and wear my watch; it is more valuable than it appears. It will stop with my last breath, and should it begin to tick again, you will know that I have once more begun to breathe. Watch it, therefore, for some space of time, that I may not be interred prematurely.

"When it has been silent for a month, put it into your own pocket. In a few hours it will begin to go again. From that moment no other must wear it. It will be a sort of guardian angel to you. While it ticks regularly, you need fear nothing. When it begins to tick very rapidly, danger threatens you. If you are about to take a journey, and are thus warned, remain at home; if while you are in the street, remain where you are until the sound is normal, or return home. Never take it to a watch-maker; it needs no regulation. It will not stop until your breath does.

"I cannot tell you why, but it has been so, and it will be so, and you will soon believe it."

The physician naturally believed that there was nothing in all this. The superstition that a man's watch often stops when he dies, without any perceptible reason, was familiar to him; but he listened gravely, promised to do as the invalid asked, and thanked him for the bequest.

However, the man lived many months longer, and died very quietly at last. He was found lying as though asleep, and the watch in the pocket of his night-robe had certainly stopped, though it had not run down.

The physician was, at least, sufficiently startled to respect the old gentleman's wishes in regard to the watch; but it remained silent, and at the end of the month he placed it in his own pocket. Exactly as the donor had said, he had not worn it twenty-four hours, before it began to tick again.

From that moment it continued to keep perfect time.

About three years from the day on which he first became its owner, it had given three manifestations of its peculiar power.

I do not know the particulars, save that by stopping in the street while the wild ticking of the watch continued, the doctor was saved from passing an old wall which fell just at the time when he would have been beneath it had he continued his walk; that the same wild ticking caused him to return home in time to save the life of one of his family, who needed instant attention; and that, obeying its warning, he did not enter a railway train, in which, an hour after, many passengers met a fearful fate.

But, by this time, not even the original possessor of the watch felt a greater confidence in it as a sort of mechanical guardian angel.

The doctor's wife also believed in it implicitly, and would not, on any account, have allowed him to leave the house without it, had she been aware of the fact.

One day, however, the hasty change of a waistcoat caused this to happen. The fact was discovered by the lady, and shortly, to her horror, she heard the watch begin to tick madly; then, to stop suddenly, with a sort of crash. The terror that this caused her was so great that she was prepared for anything, and was not astonished when her husband was shortly after brought home unconscious—his horse having taken fright at something and overturned the carriage. He did not rally, and finally the physicians pronounced him dead.

The usual solemn preparations were made; the funeral took place, and all seemed over, when, in the middle of the night, the seeming widow, who lay awake, with her eyes fixed upon the watch, which she had placed upon her pillow, heard it begin to tick again, and that with astonishing rapidity.

On the instant she felt sure that her husband was not dead, and, rising, summoned those who could aid her, proceeded to the burial place, unlocked the vault, where the coffin lay on a stone slab, and had the lid lifted.

The first glance showed a gleam of color in the doctor's face.

Wrapped in blankets, which his wife had provided, he was borne home and laid upon his bed. There he was restored to full consciousness, regained his health and lived to extreme old age.

Certainly, if this was a coincidence—as is, of course, possible—it was a most fortunate one, and no one could blame those who saw all this happen for regarding the watch with reverence and affection, and believing all that its original possessor had told them to be solemnly true, forever afterward.

A DREAM.

A curious dream that visited the sleep of a little girl, one night, seems to find its proper place here.

She was paying a visit to friends in the country, and

was in good health and spirits when she retired. Her mind was full of the rural sports that she so much enjoyed, and though she knew that her step-father was not well, she had always seen people, who were ill, recover, and resume their places in the household, and did not feel that it was a matter to trouble about.

However, no sooner did she fall asleep, than she dreamed that she was once more at home, and found the house empty.

In vain she looked for her mother, and when she ran up to the room where she had seen her step-father lying in bed—behold! the bedstead had been drawn to the centre of the room, and divested of its furniture, and to each post was tied, by a black ribbon, a great, white horse.

The next morning, her hostess took her on her knee, and gently broke the news that her step-father was dead. He had expired after the child left home, and as it was not thought expedient to summon the little girl to the funeral, it had taken place the day before— a message to that effect having been received at the country house, without the child having been aware of it.

SISTER ZELIA.

There are, in this city, many homes for poor girls, where those who have been ill, or, perhaps, in prison, are fed and taught for a certain space, and then provided with an outfit of clothing, so that they can begin an honest, working life under favorable circumstances.

On several occasions, I have taken servants from

these homes, and last year I employed a girl who told me what follows. I have only her word for it, but I see no reason why she should have invented the tale.

The home where she had been staying was under the care of a number of ladies, who devoted themselves to charitable work.

They were known to the poor only as Sister Ann—Maria—etc., etc. They wore a religious habit, and were connected with the Episcopal Church. She described them as being as good as angels, but said that there had been one amongst them, called Sister Zelia, who was better than all the rest—to whom they looked up as to some superior being.

This lady had lately departed this life, knowing that she should be greatly missed by those with whom she worked; and Jane asserted that it was a recognized fact amongst the Sisters that she often visited them. They saw her in the chapel very frequently; but her chief task was in taking charge of the unruly girls during the necessary absence of the workers still in the flesh.

Jane declared that she had heard the Sisters talk about it many times. That they said, that when the sewing class was full of troublesome persons, who had not rid themselves of old habits and were disposed to be disorderly, Sister Zelia would glide in.

The girls never saw her, but the Sisters did, and could notice her walking amongst them in her old and gentle way—and soon the ill-feeling would subside, the needles would move quietly and the faces grow amiable.

The spirit Sister would nod and smile encouragingly, and at the same time take the teacher's seat. The latter might leave the room to eat or rest, or attend to some important thing, in the full assurance that there would be no disturbance while she was absent.

"And, moreover," Jane said, "sometimes she'd open the door."

Sister —— said, that one day the door-bell had rung, and she ran down stairs to answer it, when, behold! Sister Zelia came out of the parlor and put her hand on the lock. Sister —— stepped back and made a bow—on which Sister Zelia smiled, motioned her to come forward and went into the parlor again.

"This time," Jane added, "she was so real that Sister —— forgot she was dead, for a minute."

I think that Jane believed all this implicitly.

A VIRGINIA WITCH STORY.

The story I am about to tell is one that is sometimes told by a lady in Virginia, who declares that she believes every word of it. A coarser version is in circulation amongst the negroes, who frighten each other with it of winter nights as they gather round their winter fires, smoking their corn-cob pipes.

It is interesting as proving that all the witches did not live and die in Salem, and bears a sort of second-cousinly relation to the old English ballad stories. I give it to the reader as I heard it, merely as a curiosity.

Years ago, there lived in Virginia a gentleman named McKin, who was greatly respected by all who knew him. He was rich; he was kindly; he had the good wishes of all his neighbors; he was an excellent master and a good friend. He owned a great deal of real estate, and amongst it was the finest mill property in the county. It was known as "McKin's Grist Mill," and was very valuable. Mr. McKin always kept a miller there, and, of course, the miller had his men, and a thriving business was carried on for years. Meanwhile, Mr. McKin remained a bachelor, and lived in the old family mansion with his mother and sisters, until the former died and the latter married. The people began to say that now, no doubt, Mr. McKin, himself, would marry. He was no longer young, and sundry widows were spoken of as most likely to be chosen as the future lady of the McKin house. However, neither maid nor matron of the place could flatter herself that the bachelor's attentions were "particular."

He lived alone with his large retinue of servants for a year, and at last astonished his friends by marrying a lady who was an utter stranger to every one—a very beautiful young woman, who had golden hair, great black eyes, a skin like cream, and a brown mole on her left cheek.

He gave a great supper to introduce her, and told every one that he hoped to see them often, and that the dull life he had led for some time was now at an end. His bride was admired by all. Her dress was exquisite; she sparkled with jewelry, and a magnificent cluster ring she wore on the middle finger of the right hand attracted much attention. It was, like all the rest, a gift from Mr. McKin.

The host did his best; the supper was delightful. There was a band of music from Richmond; there were roses everywhere. Mr. McKin had tried to make the affair a splendid one; but when it was over, the guests began to acknowledge to each other that they were disappointed. Why, they could not say—perhaps Mrs. McKin was cold in her manner; some people could not help being that—but they had not been happy, and in old times every one had enjoyed himself so much at the McKin's.

Then some one hinted that the house servants did not like their new lady, and liked still less her strange foreign maid, little and dark, and withered as an old monkey.

"No"; old Phœbe, the cook, had said to some one, "we-alls don' like madame's maid; we-alls don' like her. We got no right to talk about de madame, nohow; but madame's maid she jes a nigger, same as de rest, and we-alls reckon she mighty curus, mighty curus." It was plain that old Phœbe would have said the same of Mrs. McKin, had she dared to do so.

The day after the party was Saturday. Mrs. McKin professed herself weary and remained in bed until supper time. Sunday morning, however, she arose. As she was eating breakfast, her husband spoke of the hour.

"We shall have to make some haste, my dear," he said, "in order to be at church in season."

It was some time before his wife answered him; then she said, "I will not go to church to-day.'

"I am very anxious that you should, my dear," Mr. McKin said; "it will be expected of us."

"You can go alone," she answered, coldly.

"Alone! the first Sabbath after my marriage," he cried, "oh, my dear, impossible! See what I have bought for you for the occasion"—and he took from a table a small parcel, unfolded it and handed Mrs. McKin a beautiful little prayer book, bound in blue velvet, with silver clasps, and her name on the corner in silver letters. As he placed it before her, she uttered a low cry and fainted away. The maid rushed to her aid and they carried her to her room, where thenceforward she remained.

From that moment, Mr. McKin's beautiful young wife seemed to be bedridden; she never left her pillow. Mr. McKin consulted the most celebrated physicians; none of them could discover what ailed her. The maid nursed her continually. Mr. McKin was not encouraged to enter the room; he always made his wife's head ache when he spoke to her. Finally, he contented himself with a brief call of inquiry every morning. He was a very unhappy man, more desolate than in his bachelor days.

Old Phœbe began to tell strange stories to her friend, the housekeeper at the hotel.

"Mars Jack mighty nigh done broke his heart," she would say, "I's mighty sorry for Mars Jack, but we-all jes despises the madame. She sick in bed all day, but in de night, I reckon, she mighty well, yes'm she mighty well den, and she get up and dress shese'f and eat a big supper an go out ob de do', yes'm she do, an dat little chimpmunk ob a maid she go 'long wid her an day done come back jes befo' sun-up, yes'm we-all knows dat de libin truff."

"Why don't you tell you Mars Jack?" the housekeeper asked.

"Dere aint nobody daast tell *dat* yar to Mars Jack," said Phœbe; "nobody." And no one did dare; but soon it was whispered everywhere that the beautiful Mrs. McKin had a lover, whom she went to meet in the pine woods at midnight.

But there was something else that Mr. Jack McKin was to hear shortly. There was trouble at the mill, and the trouble was of a supernatural sort—the miller and his men had seen a ghost.

One by one the men had been frightened away, and the miller was alone at his post. At last he came up to the McKin mansion one day, and resigned his millership. He was reluctant to give his reasons, but finally did so. The ghosts—there were two of them—manifested themselves every night. They were not to be frightened away, and did mischief to the grain, and set fire to the mill in various places, though he had always found the flames in time to put them out. Now they threatened to kill him if he were not gone in three days.

"I am amazed to hear such a story from a white man of intelligence," was Jack McKin's comment on the tale. "Some one is evidently trying to frighten you away. Remain, and on the night they threaten to take your life, the sheriff and his men shall be with you."

Finally, the miller returned to the mill, and, at dusk, on the third day, was seen alive and well by people who came with grist. When the sheriff and his men came stealthily through the woods an hour later, the mill was perfectly dark. They lit their lanterns and went through it, calling on the miller by name, but receiving no answer, until they found him in his own room, lying on his face, a pistol in his hand, an overturned lamp beside him, dead. He had been shot through the heart.

There was no living, human being in the old mill, and for a long while no one went near it. At last, people began to say that the miller had shot himself by accident, and that the negroes had frightened him. Another miller applied for the place, and remained three days. In fact, to cut a long story short, the only other miller who dared to brave the warning that the ghost gave them all, was found dead, as the first one had been.

The mill was soon spoken of as haunted, by every one; no one would work there, and finally Mr. McKin closed it, and it was left to itself and to the ghost.

All this while Madame McKin remained an invalid, shut in her room all day, watched by her maid and talked of in whispers by her servants.

It was a tall, strong, broad-shouldered young fellow who walked up the steps of the McKin mansion one day, asked to see the master, and begged to be allowed to take charge of the grist-mill.

"I've heard the story," he said, as Mr. McKin began to explain. "I don't believe in ghosts, and they can't scare me, any way. I'm in hard luck and I'm a good miller. Trust me, and your mill shall work better than ever. You'll do me a service and I'll do you one."

In vain Mr. McKin set before him the fact that two millers had already been killed in the haunted mill; the young giant declared that he should not be, and, finally, the gentleman engaged him. The mill was opened and the miller set to work.

He took with him into the mill a bible, a revolver, and a large, sharp axe. For the first two nights he saw nothing, but heard noises like the falling of heavy millstones on the floor above, screams and groans, and oaths uttered by hideous voices. He had expected something like this, and remained in his room, reading his bible by the light of a shaded lamp.

On the third night, having heard the same noises and quietly disregarded them, his door was dashed open and a hideous form entered. It was something between a woman and a great bird of prey. It wore fluttering white robes, and had, instead of hands, great black claws. It floated toward him through the air, and behind it came another, like unto it, but smaller. The first creature swooped downward and made a clutch at the lamp—as it did so, he snatched his revolver from his belt and fired, emptying all the chambers. The strange beings vanished with wild shrieks, but in a moment they entered again. This time the largest one made a furious clutch at the lamp. As she did so, he lifted his axe above his head, and with one blow severed the hideous, black claw from what looked like a shriveled human arm; then he hurled his bible at the head of the smaller fiend. Instantly, screams, oaths and horrible curses filled the air, the strange beings vanished, and silence reigned. The black claw dropped to the table—it was such a hideous sight that the miller covered it with a cloth, that he might not see it.

He kept watch all night, and, early in the morning, Mr. McKin, who had been told that firing had been heard in the mill, came to make inquiries. The miller told his tale and Mr. McKin complimented him on his bravery. Of course, he was desirous of seeing the amputated claw, and the miller proudly drew away the cloth. Behold! there lay upon the table, not a claw, but a woman's beautiful hand—a right hand—on the middle finger of which gleamed a splendid cluster diamond ring.

At the sight of this, horror seized the miller, and Mr. McKin seemed as if about to die. He knew the hand; he knew the ring.

Then, without a word, he walked out of the mill and homeward, and into his wife's chamber. She was in bed, as usual. The maid, pale, and with a great bruise on her forehead, interposed to prevent his approach: "Madame is very ill," she said.

"Out of my way, woman," he cried, and pushed her aside; then, bending over his wife's bed, but without his usual show of tenderness, he said, sternly: "Show me your hand."

She thrust forth her left one. "The other," he said.

She uttered a scream, and he turned down the counterpane; but there was no hand to show, only a bandaged stump, from which it had been severed.

The next day, the whole country was horrified by hearing that Jack McKin, the most universally beloved and admired resident of the place, had committed suicide. He had shot himself through the brain, beside his mother's grave.

Hundreds of people attended his funeral, and most of them were real mourners.

As for Mrs. McKin and her maid, no one had seen them leave the house; they had called for neither carriage nor horses, and made no preparations for departure. The ladies' elegant wardrobe was scattered about in the greatest confusion. No care had been taken of either jewelry or money. There was blood upon the towels, and bloody stains upon the doors, and the maid's room was in the same disorder. No one ever saw either of the women again.

A few days later, a committee of grave and reverend personages went to the mill to examine the hand which the miller had kept folded in a cloth; but when they stood around the table, and with trembling hands undid the wrappings—behold! there lay before them only an immense and hideous black claw. Of this they took possession, and it was for a long time preserved in spirits in the court-house of the town. It is declared that no one, however learned in such matters, was ever able to say to what sort of creature it belonged, and that it more greatly resembled the claw of the fabled Griffin than any other thing that can be thought of.

McKin's Mills is still pointed out to strangers who visit the neighborhood. It is now a weather-stained, moss-covered ruin, which no one ever enters, and which no negro could be induced to pass after nightfall; for they believe that, exactly as the clock strikes twelve, two horrible creatures, with flaming eyes and flapping wings, are to be seen, and the largest and fiercest has but one claw.

There are hundreds of stories, as weird as this, told by the negroes of the South; but it is difficult to get into the confidence of those who remember them. The old people mistrust the motives of "white folks" who question them. They will seldom do more than to confess that for "sartin sure dey is haants and dey is witches." There can be no doubt, however, that could the material be collected, a very interesting volume of Southern folk-lore could be written. Nothing can be more certain than that most of the negroes believe in voudoo, though the mysteries of this sort of black magic are buried in the bosoms of the descendants of the Africans who were brought to this country in the old slave ships.

CHAPTER 10.

SOME CELEBRATED MEDIUMS.

MISS EDMONDS.

The first medium I ever saw was Miss Edmonds, the daughter of Judge Edmonds. I was very young at the time—many girls are still going to school at that age—though I had already been wife and widow. I was living at home in my father's house, and would not have been permitted to go alone to a public spiritual seance, or to the house of the ordinary clairvoyant, but Miss Edmonds was the friend of a friend of ours, and kindly sent me word to come to her that she might try to get some communication for me. Miss Edmonds was a lady, born and bred; to no one did she make any charge whatever. A fair woman, with large blue eyes, I remember her.

When she had closed the door of the reception room into which she invited me, we had a little chat, and I remember that she told me that she longed to see her mother and a sister, or sisters, who had passed away, but that she could never be passive enough. They appeared for an instant, faint and dim as shadows; but her agitation prevented her from communicating with them and they vanished. Words to this effect—I am not using her exact language.

She was a lovely, gentle woman, and not the person to deceive any one, even had there been the trace of a motive for it.

It was some little while before she became entranced, and strange changes passed over her face and its expression altered greatly. Then she began to speak in a strong, Irish brogue.

She had told me that she was controlled by an Irish spirit.

A message was given to me which purported to be from my husband, and she told me I had lost a little baby, and that the flowers that were placed in its dead hands were " hyacinths made of wax." This was true. In fact, I had received what a Spiritualist would consider a proof of spirit presence. The only other explanation is that she unconsciously read my mind, which is in itself sufficiently astonishing.

I am told that this lady afterward came to regard communication with spirits as a sin, and entered a convent, where she still remained when I received the information. But I do not comprehend why a devout Catholic should see any sin in such visions as those of Miss Edmonds. The Irishman who was believed by her to be her "control" was plainly a good Christian, and the advice he gave might have fallen from the lips of any pious clergyman.

I cannot remember interviewing any medium from that day until I went to Foster's seance rooms.

Though I had once met a woman who "saw things" in crystals, and who described a most peculiar person, perfectly, in a very amusing fashion.

As my experience with Charles Foster was a really astonishing thing, and sent me home positively convinced that on that occasion, at least, he was possessed of unaccountable power, I will give it in detail.

I had heard marvelous tales of Foster. I had also heard that he had been "exposed in court"; that is, that it was proven that red letters, such as often appeared upon his arm, could be produced by a trick. Doubtless they can. Perhaps he thus produced them; but that does not explain away such a fact as this: Two people arrive from the far West one morning. They have never seen Foster, but on the cars a Spiritualist had told them wonderful stories of him. They decide that this is one of the New York sights they wish to see, and that it will be worth the five dollars apiece that it will cost them. They make some changes in their dress at a hotel, dine, light their cigars and walk to Foster's rooms. They have never seen him, or he them; they are no more publicly known than any two gentlemen who have been ordinarily prosperous in business; they have told no one of their intention to visit Foster. As they walked along, they have said to each other, "What shall we ask?" and one has said, "Well, I should like to know about Bill McLane." This is a long distance from Foster's residence.

They enter the seance room. Without having been introduced by name, or having given their cards, and before they have spoken a word, Foster rolls up his shirt sleeves, walks toward them and strikes his arm briskly, and they see upon it, in bright red letters—William McLane.

"That is the man you want to know about—he is standing near you—he came in before you," he says, "you are—(so and so and so and so)," giving their names correctly, "and he says, I did not commit suicide, I fell into the water. I could have got out if it had been smooth bottom there, but I stuck in the mud, you remember."

Bill McLane, as his friends called him, was found under such circumstances as these—the account was correct. To prepare red letters to start forth on his arm, might have been easy, but what "trick" could teach Foster that William McLane was the name in the mind of these strangers, or that he was drowned in a western river.

I do not vouch for this story; but it had been told. Others, similar, had been sworn to, and the knowledge of facts was much more important than the production of red letters on human flesh.

I cannot say that, on the day on which I went to Foster's rooms, I believed any of these stories. Indeed, I had met with so many Spiritualists, who, being devout believers in the phenomena of Spiritualism themselves, felt that it was best for others to believe also, and who, not having testimony which would convince troublesome people who asked questions, were prone to add to stories they took on faith the little things they needed to win the credence of skeptics, that my trust in human testimony was shaken.

Too zealous Spiritualists tell these small white lies for your "own little good" in order that you may be as happy as they are. So do wonder-lovers for the sake of amazing you. And, as my hand was on Mr. Foster's bell, I said to myself that I was probably about to illustrate once more the adage, "a fool and his money are soon parted," by presenting a five dollar note to a clever impostor. However, I did not turn away; I entered. A number of ladies were seated about a well-furnished parlor, and a lady with white hair advanced and spoke to me. She told me that Mr. Foster was engaged at the moment; but if I could wait, he would see me soon. I had never seen the lady before, nor did she know me. The guests were chatting, and one lady, a very handsome woman, who spoke of Georgia as her home, was telling marvelous things that people she knew had heard from Mr. Foster.

After a while the lady with white hair informed me that if I chose I could write out ten or twelve questions beforehand, in order to save time by having them ready. I was full of the idea of trickery and deception, and therefore said to myself, "she will probably watch me and tell him what I write." Therefore, I took the paper she gave me, thin, white wrapping paper, and a book on which to place it, and sat down in a corner which a large piece of furniture, a sort of sideboard, fenced off from the rest of the room. It was in a dark corner, and the ladies I have mentioned sat near the window, where the lady with white hair joined them; and, assuredly, they were entirely occupied with their conversation and made no attempt to watch me.

I wrote twelve questions; the first and its answer will be amply sufficient for my purpose. In writing it,

I thought of my father, to whom I was ardently attached. I believe I adored him from the moment I opened my eyes on this world. He was stricken down in the midst of his usefulness, and with his dreams and hopes all unfulfilled, to suffer an agonizing illness of three years, of which he died before he was yet fifty years of age. He had been lost to us for ten years on the date of my visit to Charles Foster, and I am sure that they had never met; that Mr. Foster did not know me; that I had never seen any of the ladies in the parlor, and, moreover, though I thought of my father, I refrained from using his name, or any name, in the questions I wrote, or from signing them even by so much as an initial.

But I must still further preface my story in order to explain the question. I must first say that during my father's lifetime he conceived the idea of painting a panorama of the "Pilgrim's Progress." When I was a little child, I had heard him talk of it; and, while I was still a little girl, he, for a time, abandoned his regular art work in order to complete this.

If any one amongst my readers, who had the heart and eye of an artist, ever saw that panorama, I need not tell them that it was a thing of beauty, something set apart from any other work of the kind I ever saw. My father, Mr. Joseph Kyle, was a great painter, and a portrait of him, by himself, which we have at home, is as fine a head as any by the most renowned painters of the world. It is very rarely that such a man paints a panorama. The wonderful coloring, skies such as nature gives us, the delicate illustration of Bunyan's great allegory, made it unique and valuable, and not to be confounded with a pretty little panorama of the same name recently exhibited in Sunday-schools. Artists who saw my father's panorama grew enthusiastic over it. It was an ideal work of which my father had talked and dreamed, and I knew that if he retained his identity, he would not forget it. Therefore, I resolved to speak of that in my question. What I wrote was simply this:

"Dear father, will you tell me what art work you were most interested in, in 18—?" giving the year from memory.

As I wrote these words, I felt a sort of grieved contempt for myself for being in such a place at all, and had no expectation of receiving any definite answer. Moreover, I did my best to make what I had written illegible. I did not fold the paper; I rolled it into a ball, pressing it hard with my palms and making a circular motion all the while. Then I wrote the other questions, and I have regretted ever since that they were all too ill-considered to be tests, however much to the point the answers might be. In fact, I was already disgusted with the whole affair.

After all the little pellets were made the size of large pease and quite hard, I shook them in my handkerchief, mixing them so that I could not have picked out any one of them. Just then I was told that Mr. Foster was disengaged, and was ushered into a large, square room, very fresh and bright, the windows wide open, and the furniture little more than a table, some chairs, a what-not full of books and the mantel decorations.

It struck me at first as rather unconventional in the medium to wear no coat; but I soon remembered that he was obliged to roll up his sleeves in order to exhibit the red letters which appeared upon his arm. He did not at first ask me to be seated, or take a seat himself, but, standing near the window, folded back his shirt sleeve, held his left arm rigidly extended and struck it thrice between the wrist and elbow with the palm of his right hand. Waiting a moment, he repeated this process, but nothing came of it.

"Sometimes names appear on my arm," he said. "But they won't come this time." He seemed disappointed and walked toward the table, pulling down the sleeves and buttoning the wristbands.

A photograph album lay there; he handed it to me, asking if I would like to look at it, opening it at a picture of himself, with a very solemn looking "spook" holding a white wreath over his head. I returned it with the words: "I know how those are made." I thought I did then; I am not so sure now. How often I recall the remark of an old German, to whom my husband had just taught some useful thing he did not know before, as to the management of a horse.

"Vell, vell, so longer as a man lives, so more he finds, by gracious goodness, out."

At least we find "out" that we know very little. Yet, to this day, those "spook" pictures savor of fraud, and I cannot see why a man, who could really do such wonderful things, exhibited them.

Suffice it to say that, as Mr. Foster placed the book on the what-not, laughing as he did so, I was ready to turn in disgust from the room and leave him to deceive others. However, I sat down at the table and he took a seat opposite me. He asked me if I had "written any questions?" and I produced my dozen little balls. He took them from me, touched them to his forehead for the briefest space of time and tossed them back upon the table.

As they touched his forehead, he had read aloud the questions I had asked, as rapidly as though they had been printed and lying before him. He did *not* unroll them, exchange them or perform any trick whatever. When all were read, he said: "An answer comes to this one"—pushing one toward me with a pencil. "Dear father, will you tell me what art work you were most interested in, in 18—?"

As he spoke, I unrolled the paper and found within the question he repeated, very much rubbed and smudged, to be sure, and difficult to decipher by any stranger not having a key to it. I now felt interested; for, if my salvation depended upon it, I could swear that there was not a possibility of deception. He had read what was written by other than the usual means.

He took a pencil from his pocket, and paper lay on the table. He drew it toward him, then pushed it back.

"Sometimes," he said, "they give me my answer in the form of a picture—that will be done this time." He pushed back his chair and looked toward the wall of the room: "Ah!" said he, "I see the figure of an old man in a brown gown, with a book in his hand."

"He fancies he is describing my father," I thought,

But the next thing he said was: "Why, it is old Bunyan. The book in his hand is Bunyan's 'Pilgrim's Progress.' Does he say your father illustrated the 'Pilgrim's Progress?' No, no! that is not what he says—your father painted a panorama of the 'Pilgrim's Progress'—you ask him about that;" and then he gave me, after a little pause, my father's name, Joseph Kyle.

Now, even if he had known my father, it is not likely that he would have hit upon this panorama to speak of, since panorama painting was not my father's specialty. He was known as a portrait painter, and an historical painter. There were other things that would have been selected by a shrewd deceiver as being my father's work.

Then Mr. Foster did not know whose daughter I was, and I had never seen him before nor been in any society where he was personally known. I could be positively certain, also, that I had never met any of those ladies who were in the parlor.

Later, he told me that he saw the spirit of a deceased friend, who introduced me by my full name. But the lady had recently passed away, and was well known to the public, so his knowledge of her name proved nothing.

And now let me ask if, per possibility, Mr. Foster knew and recognized me, and was able, by some juggling trick, to produce any one's name upon his arm, why had he not done so? He had had ample time for preparation.

In manner, I thought Mr. Foster honest and simple

to a degree. He seemed deeply interested in what he saw, and had not the air of one playing a part. However, the only convincing point was the truth of his replies to my questions. He might have deceived my senses, but what he told me was not within his knowledge.

The other pellets of paper were read in the same manner; I unrolled them on the spot, and mind-reading did not cover the ground, since I could not have told one from the other. In all cases he gave me definite replies; but I had not written them with judgment, they were not test questions, save to myself—a fact which I now regret.

Of course, only those who had experience of the same kind, with the same man, ever would believe that I told this story exactly as it happened. That he unrolled the pellets as the prestidigitateur would, was the usual idea; or, that I chattered to the ladies in the front room, and that he got his information thus; that he knew my father, and had the panorama of the "Pilgrim's Progress" stored away in his mind in case I should come to one of his seances—this is the unlikeliest of all; as I have said, my father was a painter of portraits and historical pictures.

He stepped outside of his usual line when he painted this panorama. Foster would have been much more likely to mention something else had he known my father.

I never saw this medium again. My impression is that he left New York very shortly and never again held seances in that city.

The Fox sisters have been public property ever since the epoch of the Rochester Knockings; nor can I remember any time when some one had not investigated and exposed, *in the papers*, their whole system of making the raps with the toe-joints; yet, still, they continued to rap and to be paid for rapping.

Once, I remember, Mr. Cafferty, the artist, came into my father's studio and told the following story:

He was painting a portrait of one of the Fox girls—I am not sure which—and, as she posed, he said to her:

"Miss Fox, I have never heard any of your famous raps; do you think you could make your spirits rap for me?"

"I can try, Mr. Cafferty," Miss Fox replied. "Where will you have the rap?"

He designated a door which opened into an adjoining studio occupied by another artist; and she arose, and, holding back her skirt, touched the tips of her fingers to the panels. In an instant the knocks came.

"They were not little taps," I remember Mr. Cafferty said; "they were like the blows of a sledge-hammer." It was impossible for her to have made them with her toes, he went on to say, and that the wood vibrated under them.

In 1886, I think, I made an appointment with Mrs. Kane to come to my house for an evening.

She came. Chairs were placed around a table and some writing done, nothing convincing, but we heard positive raps. I *felt* them distinctly upon my chair, Mrs. Kane's hands being on the table and her feet set close together in full view upon the floor. Such blows as could be made with a tack-hammer. I at that time sat next to Mrs. Kane. I changed my seat, putting a gentleman, one of our family, next to her, and two more blows came, really uncomfortable ones, upon my back. The sounds were quite audible elsewhere; they appeared to fall on the table, or the wall, or the floor.

Before leaving us, Mrs. Kane stood near an open door, held back her skirts so that her feet could be seen, and, standing at the length of her arm, touched the tips of her fingers to the panels.

Raps, not loud, but strong, came upon the door, and our hands being upon it, felt the reverberation.

The blows upon my own person were, however, the most singular.

I believe Mrs. Kane, before her death, made public confession of deception; but I should be glad to know how "her toes" could strike my back in a lighted room, where I was one of a tableful of persons, all on the watch for deception, none of them having any faith in the rappings. No proof whatever of spirit presence was given; but I believed and still believe the raps to be phenomenal.

CHAPTER II.

ABOUT BABIES.

Do you remember William Wordsworth's beautiful poem, Intimations of Immortality?—let me quote the fifth verse:

> "Our birth is but a sleep and a forgetting,
>   The soul that rises with us, our life's star,
> Hath had elsewhere its setting,
>   And cometh from afar;
> Not in entire forgetfulness,
> And not in utter nakedness,
> But trailing clouds of glory do we come
> From God, who is our home:
> Heaven lies about us in our infancy!
> Shades of the prison-house begin to close
>   Upon the growing boy;
> But he beholds the light, and whence it flows
>   He sees in it his joy;
> The youth who daily farther from the east
> Must travel, still is nature's priest,
> And by the vision splendid
> Is on his way attended;
> At length the man perceives it die away,
> And fade into the light of common day."

In the author's note to this poem, Mr. Wordsworth, speaking of the belief in a prior state of existence, remarks:

"Let us bear in mind that, though the idea is not advanced in Revelation, there is nothing to contradict it, and the fall of man presents an analogy in its favor.

"Accordingly, a pre-existent state has entered into the popular creeds of many nations, and, among all persons acquainted with classic literature, is known as an ingredient in Platonic philosophy."

This is not exactly the Theosophical idea of incarnation, but it approaches it.

The re-incarnation theory rather frightens me. I like better to think that once this world's troubles are over, I shall go to a happier shore. But plainly, things in general were not arranged to suit my particular fancy, and it may be that I have been ever so many people, and shall be ever so many more. I used to say, in my childhood, that I knew I had once been a little angel, because I remembered flying as well as I now remember anything that happened in my babyhood, and I have proved to older people that I could remember many occurrences that transpired when I was ten months old.

I have described to my mother a house, whence we moved when I was that age, and especially how my father taught me to walk—on a blue box, a long one, which stood for a while in the back garden, and which I had never seen since, or heard spoken of.

I also described a great ivy vine, growing over a church wall, and an old-fashioned hydrant, in an openway behind the garden, and told the name of the grocer the family dealt with—"Stewart"—which I remembered because I liked the sugar-crackers bought there, and had heard people say—"when you go to Stewart's, get some crackers for Mamie."

I can distinctly recall the effort of balancing myself,

and my fear of falling—a perfect terror—so that I would not step alone for a long while, though I have all my life, since, delighted in the exercise of walking, as some people do in riding, others in dancing.

But, while I remember places, people and occurrences, I remember my emotions best, and I can tell you just how a baby feels.

A baby feels more strongly than a grown person, especially when it is very young. It cannot remember much before ten months; but perhaps its feelings are more intense at one month—one week—one day. Its poor, useless little body cannot express anything, but I am not sure what it may be feeling—I do not say *thinking*, remember. Its shrieks may be expressions of a woe unutterable, its smiles of an angelic joy. I know that a baby a year old can love as men and women cannot. How it loves its mother! "Natural instinct"—you say. No; it is pure love. I loved my mother, my father and my grandmother, intensely. When, in the evening, father took me on his knee, great waves of bliss used to sweep over me—actual currents of joy. We all felt that in childhood, when father held us in his arms—we have spoken of it together.

A baby feels intense love, intense fear, intense longing for the presence of those dear to it, only generally it forgets all about it later. It has no anticipation; it lives in the present. It feels, at new objects, astonishment not to be expressed by any words of mine, and it wants to know—oh, how it wants to know everything!

I was supposed to be different from other babies of my age, because I talked glibly at a year, and asked questions by the hundred. But it was only that I could talk, while they were yet dumb.

"How did the ladies get into the cages?" was one important question in my mind, at twelve months. I thought of it before I asked it. I remember pondering it carefully, and putting it to every one. No one knew what I meant; people thought I called the canary bird "a lady," but I knew birds from women.

I asked again and again. At last they discovered that, when I was taken out, I saw people looking from the upper windows, which had green blind shutters. I could not think how they got there, and my mother taught me, with some trouble, the mystery of stairs and windows, showing me the windows from outside of the house, and then taking me up to look out of them.

No astronomer, who should, some day, see through a telescope all the mysteries of Mars, could be more delighted with his knowledge than I.

I could write a little book, all by itself, of my memories from the age of one year to that of five; and I believe we come into the world with all our emotions about us, not our passions.

At least we are not aware of them, until they are brought to light by the events and conditions of lives. But the spirit is there, and what belongs to it, and, most of all, love. Take that comfort to your hearts, mothers. That little creature in your arms, for whom you have suffered, for whom you gladly sacrifice your ease, your repose, pleasant intercourse, many things every day—that darling little baby of yours is not merely a little animal. It loves you already. It cannot show you that love in any way, as yet, but you feel it. That is why a poor working woman will sometimes say—"it rests me so to take baby," when some one, who does not know what an infant can be to a mother, feels that it must be only an additional burden, another trouble in her weary life.

As for memory of a past existence, which some people believe they have, I never had any, except that fancy of flying, which seemed to me a positive memory, and that I used to fly up above the earth through the sky.

One day, at five years of age, I attempted to give an exhibition of this power, which I felt sure I still possessed, to a younger sister, who doubted my statement.

She sat at the foot of the garret stairs, which I ascended, and I flew from the top, flapping my arms, since I had no wings.

The result astonished me. Instead of floating gently down, as I expected to do, I came to the floor with a crash, to the consternation of the family.

Several cuts and bruises remained to remind me of the adventure. But I suffered more from disappointment—I remembered that it had been so delightful to fly.

I have a friend whose baby girl always knew when her father was coming home. He traveled constantly and often arrived without warning; but whenever the little child said "papa is coming"—the mother knew that he was near at hand.

Before she could talk plainly, the tiny girl would go to the window, insist on having the door opened, and declare:

"Papa toming!" If some one said—"no dear, papa is far away," she would stamp her little foot and say—"yes, yes, papa toming," and it was always so.

A BABY GHOST-SEER.

Lately, I have heard a story of a baby whose father died a few weeks ago. The family live in New York State. My informant tells me that the little one declares that every night papa comes and plays with her, "just as he used to."

She tells of their romps, and what papa does and says. The mother believes it true; so do her friends. The persons who tell the story, say that Mrs. —— tries to lie awake and see the miracle, but that she can never do so, for heavy sleep always falls upon her, and nothing happens while she is awake.

I have only heard this from strangers; but they certainly believed the tale they told.

CHAPTER 12.

PLANCHETTE.

From such memories as these Planchette cannot be omitted.

Queer little Planchette, to which one involuntarily accords such personality as a family sewing-machine, or clock, or typewriter possesses in one's fancy. I remember well how I heard of her. At a certain social meeting, a lady sitting near me said:

"I suppose you have seen Planchette? I have such a funny story about Planchette."

I did not even know what Planchette was, and as the name implied that it was a little board of some sort, I fancied it to be a game, and made some remark to that effect. My neighbor then explained what it was and how it was manipulated, and told me that a very well-bred and exceedingly pious family of her acquaintance—the father a clergyman of the Universalist Church—had bought one and that it answered all their questions correctly. That they were infatuated with it and played with it every evening, until, at last, it "began to swear," and, in the end, used such shocking language that they were obliged to banish it. If I remember rightly, they came to believe that some evil being, if not Satan himself, supervised this remarkable toy, and to feel actually afraid of it.

I, however, secretly believed that the wicked spirit dwelt in some living person whose fingers touched the little board, and I straightway bought a Planchette of my own and conveyed it home with me.

With the enthusiasm of youth we gathered around the table, on which were spread sheets of brown paper, and squealed with delight when our three-legged mystery began to walk about on its roller-skates. At first it made long loops, pot hooks, and "wiggle-waggles." Nothing else expresses my meaning, so forgive me for coining a word. And, at last, when any four hands were upon it, it would "write," but not for any one person. Our Planchette assuredly only once became profane. On one occasion it used a big, big D, but apologized in the most abject manner and promised to behave better in the future. But, alas! it was untruthful. It told us many solemn falsehoods.

That this one was dead; that that building was in flames; that all sorts of public catastrophes had occurred, without having the slightest foundation for its tales. Reproached, it would laugh, writing "ha-ha-ha" upon the paper, or standing on two legs and bringing down the other rapidly, with a wild "rat-tat-too."

We were, none of us, intentionally deceiving the rest: we were too honest, too much in earnest, we would have scorned to do it for the sake of fun; but Planchette gave us many hearty laughs before it began to write under what one might call a *nom de plume*, always signing itself "Charlie," and becoming simply absurd. It conveyed to us the impression of a young, half-educated, wholly unreliable man, or perhaps a big boy. It was flippant always; it continually acted the same role, and never took on any other character.

Occasionally it told us the truth. As I wish to do this always, I shall be obliged to state exactly how this was.

Planchette, after losing all credit for veracity, suddenly uttered a little prophecy which "came true," and, when complimented on this, wrote:

"Oh, yes; when Mastadon on the chimney sees a thing it is always so."

"What is Mastadon on the chimney?" we inquired. But Planchette would not explain. However, when "Mastadon on the chimney sees this" was written by way of preface, the always unimportant prophecy was fulfilled.

Absurd as it was, this is a proof to our minds that none of us even involuntarily moved Planchette; the mysterious being, "Mastadon on the chimney," was the outgrowth of an imagination, which belonged to none of us individually.

Nothing valuable enough to record was ever written that I can remember, except that once an address, that none of us were conscious of knowing, was given, and that once Planchette wrote—"Mastadon on the roof says that Snowtop is coming this afternoon."

We knew no one called Snowtop; it is not a likely name.

Finally, we decided that Charlie alluded to some one with white hair. He said "no."

"With a white hat, then?"

Still "no"; then was added, "her name is Snowtop," and Planchette became mute.

That afternoon a young lady named Whitehead called, a Miss Whitehead, and when Planchette wrote for us again, these words were scribbled: "Well, she came; didn't she? Whitehead and Snowtop are the same."

At last came a period of stupid sameness, trivial jokes. Plainly the ministering power which possessed Planchette was not improving, mentally or morally, and then the brass legs grew loose and finally came off, and it was put away and never mended.

I think that most people who possessed a Planchette will remember that theirs came to some such end.

But there is no need of the little board. Let any two people shut themselves up in a quiet place, one of them holding a pencil of soft lead, and having beneath it some soft paper, suitable for the purpose, the other grasping the wrist of the hand that holds the pencil, and probably in a short time one will say, "are you pulling my hand?" and the other, "certainly you are pulling mine?" and whatever happens with Planchette will happen without it, and usually much more.

I do not say that all couples will experience this; but many will. There will be scribbling, followed by writing of more or less importance. You need to be as passive as possible and to trust each other implicitly.

I am not sure that any valuable proof of anything has been thus attained, and I am not sure that it has not been, either.

It may be self-delusion, where people are given to deluding themselves. A wicked person could easily deceive another, but all the grins of ridicule, all the sneers of contempt do not do away with the fact that the hands of two persons thus joined will, without conscious physical or mental exertion on the part of either, write intelligent sentences.

I have a theory of my own which I have never heard advanced—it is this: That there is a certain sort of telegraphic communication between ourselves and those who are inhabitants of other worlds or other spaces.

As, like everybody else, I have no knowledge of the subject, and can only theorize, I cannot express myself exactly, but I mean this: That, wherever they are, they have learned to communicate with us in that fashion—that they are not in the room, touching our wrists, but that they send messages by electric currents.

That we often do not comprehend them, also that they make mistakes, is certain; so do ordinary telegraph operators; but it seems certain that experiments are being made which will result in undoubted telegraphic communication with the spirit world. The impression is, in my opinion, made upon the brain of what might be called the "operator" at this end of the line. It is certain that where people are not deluding themselves, or trifling, a loud noise, sometimes even a cough, or the movement of a chair, will put an end to the writing on the spot, and even cause the persons who hold the pencil to turn faint.

That, by this pencil-writing, things occurring at a distant place are sometimes communicated, I think I have proof. In one case, persons holding the pencil wrote this:

"Poor M. Oh, dear! She has fallen from her chair—some one must go to her or she will die. She has fainted." Then, after a pause: "K says: 'Will she never come to?' M has hurt her knee. She is unconscious. She will get well, but K is frightened. K says: 'Oh, dear me! Oh, dear me!'"

I was present when two ladies received this communication. The original paper on which the words were written has come into my hands, and I copy it. There were four or five witnesses to the fact that it was written as I say.

Full names were given, and the persons they belonged to resided in Virginia, while the writers were in New York City.

Two weeks later came a letter from "K," which contained an account of an accident which had occurred to the lady whose first name began with M—stating that, two weeks before the date at the head of the note paper, "M" had slipped down two steps that lead from a certain upper room into the passage. That she hurt her knee; but, thinking the pain would pass, sat down in a rocking-chair and began to sew. However, the pain increased to such a degree that, before long, she fainted away, and must have been unconscious for some little time when the fact was discovered.

"I thought that we should never bring her to herself," wrote "K"—"and her knee was very badly injured."

Now, you may think me silly for not considering that a coincidence. I should think myself very foolish if it did not prove to me that—(excuse me, Shakespeare, I'll never do it again)

"There are more things in Heaven and earth," than we have been in the habit of believing. For that I have not in any way embellished the story I have just told—I solemnly swear.

CHAPTER 13.

COLONEL DEYER'S WELL.

In August, 1892, the reports concerning a certain well on the property of Colonel Deyer, of Virginia, so interested the managers of the *Herald*, that they sent a special reporter to the spot to investigate the matter.

This gentleman, having entered upon the work with the intention of exposing the fraud, became convinced that it was no fraud whatever, but a genuine phenomenon—and so reported in an exhaustive article in the *Herald*, which was afterward extensively copied. As I shall copy the communication, I need say nothing more just here than that Miss Lizzie Deyer, a daughter of Colonel Deyer, discovered, by mere accident, that by holding a mirror over the surface of the well, one could see arising from its depths, the faces of human beings, as well as curious objects of all sorts, and that the faces were recognized as those of the departed by many neighbors, and by thousands who poured in from all quarters to see the marvel for themselves.

We discussed the matter in the family, and some of the gentlemen were of the opinion that it was simply a clever story, without foundation, in fact. I felt sure that this was not so, and took the liberty of writing to Colonel Deyer, telling him that I possessed all the natural curiosity of a daughter of Eve, and could not refrain from asking how much of the wonderful tale was true. The result of my letter was a most courteous reply from Colonel Deyer, and also, a little later, a letter from Miss Deyer, which I give my readers as being valuable attestation from persons of refinement and education, as well as of good social position, to the truth of phenomena, which the great majority of readers would simply consider too absurd to believe.

HANDSOM'S DEPOT, VA.,
KILDARE MANOR,
10-18-92.

MRS. MARY KYLE DALLAS,
 MY DEAR MADAME:
Pardon delay in response to yours of the 11th inst. A press of business and absence from home are my best excuses to so distinguished a lady as yourself.

Now, as to the "haunted well," none of us consider it haunted, but merely a freak of nature, a phenomenon, if you please, but, frankly, beyond my ken or that of the thousands who have witnessed its more than strange *antics*.

I assure you, the report in the *Herald* was not concocted in said *Herald* office, but was written by a Mr. H——, a reporter of said paper. Said H—— was sent here by the *Herald* to investigate. I met him at Norfolk, Va., my old home. I was introduced to him by R. C. Murray, Esq., editor of the Norfolk *Landmark*. I was questioned by a party of gentlemen in said *Land-mark* office, among whom was said H——, who laughingly said he "would like to come down and expose the fraud." I gave him *carte blanche*, and in a few days, to my astonishment, down he came, and, lo! as he stated, "the half had not been told."

Now, I have no explanation to give—all my theories are exploded; but the well is here, and has a solid foundation in *fact*, as well as a mystery in *doubt*. It is no advertising dodge—I have never charged a stiver to any one to look, and the well is not for sale, tho' I should be pleased to have some enterprising Yankee remove it, *even* to *Chicago*.

I only wish I had time to give you a succinct acc't of all its doings, but time forbids; however, if you should want a full description, my daughter, Lizzie Lee Deyer, if you wish to address her, will take pleasure in gratifying the curiosity of a daughter of Eve, she being closely allied to that noble degree. With many apologies for this rambling scrawl, I remain with sentiments of highest esteem,

Your ob't servant, &c.,

JNO. J. DEYER.

KILDARE MANOR,
HANDSOM'S, VA.

MRS. MARY KYLE DALLAS,

DEAR MADAME:

Your letter in reference to the "well" was rec'd a few days ago, & I will gladly give you an account of same so far as I am capable.

I have only one correction to make in the report which appeared in the N. Y. *Herald;* that is: the mirror was held *face* to the water instead of back of mirror to water.

It is held *perfectly flat* over the surface of the water & sometimes it is half an hour or more before an object will appear, then again they will come *faster* than a person can count.

Out of the *thousands* who have visited the "well," I have found only one (that a very old lady) that could see nothing.

A friend of mine was here to see the "well," a day or so ago, & she called for a person to appear, & in less than *two seconds* his face was seen, *life size* & as *natural* as I *ever* saw him look. I will say again, that the story in the N. Y. *Herald* was a *true* one & it would be impossible for me to give you a more definite account. Hoping you will pardon my delay in answering your letter,

    I am
      very sincerely,
        LIZZIE LEE DEYER.

A HAUNTED WELL.

[From the columns of the Sunday *Herald*, October, 1892.]

There is something new under the sun. At all events, that's how it strikes most people who have seen it. It has been discovered at Kildare, Handsom's Station, Southampton County, Va., where, according to the proverb, truth is sometimes found at the bottom of a well. Third party politics and Colonel J. Deyer's well are close competitors for public attention in Southampton just now. Perhaps I should put Colonel Deyer's well first: for, after the election is over, the well will be the only thing talked about, as it was before the conventions were held. It is good evidence of the remarkable nature of the well that it should divide interest with politics, for Virginia is one of the doubtful States, and feels her responsibility.

Last May—to be precise, May 2—the wonderful properties of the well were discovered, and its fame has been growing ever since.

A few days ago, upward of three thousand people visited the well and saw all manner of uncanny things in it. They all swear they did, at any rate, and, what is more, believe what they say. I heard of the well in Norfolk, some fifty miles away, and was assured by Ex-Congressman George Bowden that he had seen the face of his father reflected in the water of the well in broad daylight. Mr. Kenton Murray, of Norfolk, who occupies the position of Secretary to Governor McKinney, told me that he had met and talked with a number of people who had visited Colonel Deyer's farm and had seen in the waters of the well the faces of relatives who were dead, coffins, and other things not pleasant to contemplate. Mr. S. S. Nottingham, the publisher of the Norfolk *Landmark*, confirmed the statements made by Mr. Murray and Colonel Bowden.

HOW DISCOVERED.

A few days afterward, I met Colonel Deyer, who, after awhile, reluctantly told me how the peculiar properties of the well were discovered, and, evidently nettled at my look of incredulity, said—" I shall be pleased to have the representative of the *Herald* come out to Kildare and investigate the matter thoroughly."

PLAINLY VISIBLE.

Colonel Deyer has a war record, too, and his title is a genuine one. For four years he fought on the Confederate side and often in the thickest of the fray. I did not question his veracity; but the old saying holds true, " seeing is believing," and I at once resolved to see the well for myself. I took the Seaboard and Roanoke Railroad from Norfolk, and devoted two days to an examination of the well.

I arrived at Kildare after a drive of a mile through the woods, during all of which I was regaled with stories of the peculiar things the driver had seen in the well. At the station I had the same experience. The station agent and a helper were all witnesses to the uncanny things the well made visible.

Colonel Deyer was not expecting me, because I had not telegraphed my arrival; but he welcomed me, and, in response to my asking to be shown the well, at once called his daughter, and, together with his wife, we proceeded to the well, which was situated about sixty feet from the house and off to one side. A colored servant, who stood near, looked in the well with us, and, as Miss Deyer held the mirror, he exclaimed:

" Foah Gawd, dere's a bottle ! "

" What kind of a bottle ? " I asked.

" A green bottle wid silber on de top on it."

He was right. Faintly gleaming on the surface of

the water, but distinctly visible, I saw a champagne bottle appear and then mysteriously sink into the depths of the well. The rest of the party saw the same things. The bottle was only one of a hundred objects inanimate and animate that appeared on the surface of the well during the forty-eight hours I spent examining it.

FICTION BEATEN.

The sorcerer who summons up "spirits from the vasty deep," in fiction is discounted in this instance by a young Virginia beauty, who brought up flowers, jewels, bottles, coffins, visions of old ladies and young ones, venerable men and smooth-faced boys, hands with blood dripping from their wounds, bodies of dead men and women, and other queer sights that few, perhaps, will believe can be seen in the well, unless, as I did, they see them for themselves.

But Miss Deyer is not the only person who causes faces and other things to be seen on the surface of the water. Others do it as well as she. That proves that it is not the girl who is haunted.

It is a curious fact that the faces and objects which appear in the well can only be seen in the daylight, and, the brighter the sun is shining, the more distinct they become. In all the haunted houses, I remember, utter darkness was essential before the ghosts would condescend to roam around and clank chains and do other blood-curdling things.

Colonel Deyer's well is just an ordinary well, such as

you find on almost every farm in Virginia, similar in appearance to fifty-one other wells on the plantation. The other wells, however, will not reveal a face. I tried them all, and so have others. The causes that bring these curious shapes to the surface of the water in the "spook well," whatever they may be, are missing in all other wells on the farm. I cannot explain why it is so, but just have to give it up, as I did fifty theories that suggested themselves to me during the hours I spent peering down into the well, climbing down into the well and examining every inch of ground for mirrors and other devices known to tricksters and so-called mediums.

PASSING STRANGE.

I left Kildare, considerably more astonished than when I arrived. The story of an old gentleman who, after listening to a tough yarn of which the narrator said, "it is true, I saw it myself," replied, "well, I must believe it, then; but I would not believe it if I saw it myself," occurred to me. I saw the well myself; I saw the things I have described therein; but I am utterly unable to account for them.

One of the faces was that of the old gentleman with a skull-cap. I saw it as distinctly as I have seen my own countenance in my mirror.

"Dr. Tudor," said Mrs. Deyer, and "Dr. Tudor," echoed Miss Grace Petit, of Norfolk, one of the party engaged in looking in the well at the time.

"Describe Dr. Tudor," I said.

She gave me a description of him, which, in the most minute particulars, corresponded to the face that appeared in the well.

Imagination plays a large part in these sort of sights, and to make sure that what I saw was not influenced by the exclamations of people about the well, I had the group write on a piece of paper a description of what each member saw in the well.

There was a startling correspondence between them all.

"I see a white coffin"; "I see an old man looking at a white coffin"; "I see a coffin and an old man," were the words they wrote. What I saw was a white coffin, with a figure of an old man looking down into it. In a minute, the coffin passed away from the shadow on the water, and Miss Petit said:

"I wish it would come back with the lid off."

"Look!" screamed Mrs. Deyer There was the coffin, with the elliptical lid off, and under the glass could be distinguished the face and shoulder of a young girl. The sight was too much for the nerves of Miss Petit, and, with a little sigh and a shudder, she sank fainting to the ground.

All this time Miss Deyer had been holding the glass. I took it and, holding the back of the mirror toward the water, awaited developments. Then a hand, holding a Calla lily, rose from the bottom of the well and remained in sight a full minute.

They were not such "pictures" as imaginative people can see in a wood-fire, or in clouds, but much more definite.

During that afternoon, a great many faces appeared. Once, the back of a negro man, who had apparently been flogged, with the gashes bleeding, was the spectacle presented. There was something very peculiar about some of these visions. I noticed, for instance, that the head and shoulders of a man or woman would appear in one position, go away and re-appear again in half a dozen different positions. A profile view would be presented, a rear view, a front view, and top view, even. It seemed as if a recognition was eagerly sought. I noticed that the flesh generally exhibited the peculiar appearance presented by the skin of drowned people.

Miss Deyer, who has acted as medium for most of the people who have visited the well, scouts the idea that she alone can get the phantom faces in the well, and I fancy she is right.

I noticed that, when Miss Petit acted as medium, her hands trembled so that nothing could be distinguished.

The use of a mirror might lead some to suppose the pictures seen in the water were reflections from objects lying about the ground or place. I thought so, too, until I held the mirror below the edge of the square box that surrounds the well, totally shutting everything outside of it, and still the aquatic visions appeared. I thought perhaps it was the mirror that did the trick, so I procured a piece of window-glass and covered it with dark cloth, and went to the well at eight o'clock in the morning and tried it with the same results. The morning experiment was private.

As Colonel Deyer's story of the well is the best one,

I repeat it as he told it in the presence of Mr. Murray, Mr. Blain and Mr. Nottingham.

"The first of last May," said Colonel Deyer, "our house servant, Susan, said to my daughter, Miss Lizzie, 'you know, Miss Lizzie, if you takes a looking-glass on the first of May and goes to the well and holds the mirror over the well, back down, the face of your future husband will appear on the surface of the water.'

"That is an old superstition in Virginia, you know. Mrs. Deyer and Miss Lizzie laughed at the notion and dismissed it from their minds. The following day, Monday, however, Susan started to the well to draw a pail of water at noon, when Miss Lizzie picked up a mirror and followed her. Laughing, at the time, at what she regarded as the absurdity of the thing, she held the mirror in the position indicated, and Susan looked into the depths of the well at the same time. In an instant, she and her mother declare, they saw a hand wearing a diamond ring steal across the patch of shadow thrown on the surface of the water by the face of the mirror, and, in alarm, Miss Lizzie dropped the glass into the well. They fished the mirror out, and spent that afternoon holding the mirror over the well, and saw a number of things—faces of people, flowers and a beautiful white casket.

COULD FIND NO EXPLANATION.

"I was away from home at the time, in Richmond, and, when I returned, a few days later, my wife and daughter told me of the occurrence.

"I laughed at the story, exactly as you gentlemen are doing now, but did not laugh when, that afternoon, my daughter took the mirror, and, proceeding to the well, held it in the position described and bade me look. In a minute or so, a shadowy something appeared on the surface of the water, apparently rising from the bottom of the well, and I distinctly recognized the face of a neighbor who had been dead for two years. I looked around to see if my wife and daughter were playing tricks on me, but saw they were just as much startled as myself. All that afternoon I spent looking in the well and saw a number of objects. I am not superstitious and I do not believe in spirits, so I tried to find a natural explanation of the things I found in the well. Every theory that I advanced was in turn exploded, and I am just as much in the dark to-day as I was six months ago.

"The negroes about the place spread the story in the neighborhood, and the neighbors began to come to see the well, and from them the news of the queer sights to be seen got carried all about—over into North Carolina, for instance—until, lately, people drive from miles around, some coming a distance of fifty miles just to see the faces and things in the well. All this is a great source of annoyance to me, for the well is the one situated nearest the house, and we have not lived in comfort since the facts about the well got out."

Colonel Deyer told the story in a way that impressed me with his entire truthfulness and sincerity. He evidently believed what he said. If there was any humbug about the well, he was no party to it.

The well itself is the one, as stated before, that supplies the household with drinking water; it is supplied with water by eight springs and generally has about eight or ten feet of water in it. When I was there, the depth of water measured just ten feet; above that to the top of the well the distance was twenty-two feet; the diameter of the well is three and a half feet. So clear is the water that the white sand bottom can be plainly seen when the sun is shining. I saw the bottom distinctly, and noted a few things that had fallen into it. The well has been cleaned every year, and the time for cleaning the well is at hand now; but, Colonel Deyer says—"if that well is cleaned, I will have to do it myself. There is not a servant on the plantation that will go near that well alone, and, as to going in it, no money would induce them to make the venture."

As I drove away, the owner of Virginia's sensation said—"if you meet any skeptical people, send them along; I shall be only too glad to meet the person who will clear up the mystery."

Here seems to be an opportunity for the Society of Psychical Research.

CHAPTER 14.

THE STORY OF MRS. V.

There once resided in the City of New York one Mrs. V, a lady of vigorous mind, capable and practical, a widow, at the head of a family of sons and daughters, for many years. She has but recently departed this life, and I knew her to the last. Her disease was consumption; it in no way interfered with her mental powers. To the last, she was capable of managing her own affairs, was actually conscious until the moment of dissolution and tried to comfort her children by smiles and motions of her hand after she was unable to speak —the last person to suspect of hallucinations or freaks of the imagination, and in no one of her many illnesses was she ever, for a moment, delirious. I tell you this to give its full weight to the following anecdote.

Young Henry G—— was a near neighbor of the family, and regarded by them as almost one of themselves. They took a great interest in him, and he was very fond of Mrs. V, who took the place his lost mother would have held in his life.

For some years after reaching manhood and entering into business, Henry gave his friends reason to hope the best for him; but, in a moment of weakness or temptation, he betrayed a pecuniary trust. According to the young man's explanation, it was the old story of borrowing money, with the intention of returning it before the loss was discovered; but his crime was detected at once, and, though his employer was lenient and did not cause his arrest, he was dismissed without reference, and lost true and kind friends, who would have advanced his interests.

To the V family, he confided the whole truth, and, while they blamed, they were as kind as possible.

About this time, Mrs. V was taken very ill and confined to her room, and on Sunday, when Henry came to the house, was not able to see him. He himself seemed ill and in a strange state, and the young V's, who, naturally, supposed his stupefied manner to be the result of the trouble he had brought upon himself, were obliged to help him home to his boarding place. They were inexperienced and did not observe how really ill he was.

The next morning he was found dead in his bed, and the physicians declared that he died of a slow poison, which he must already have taken when he visited his friends, the V's.

He had spoken of death as a release from misery, and there could be no doubt that he had deliberately committed suicide.

These events caused much sorrow in the V family, and Mrs. V regretted that she had not been able to talk to Henry on those terrible last days of his life, as she might have given him a little hope and comfort, and, perhaps, have prevented the commission of the last fatal deed.

It was before the day of the young man's funeral,

that Mrs. V's daughter entered her mother's room, and found her awake and somewhat agitated.

"Henry G—— has been here, my dear," she said.

"Why, mother, have you forgotten that Henry is dead?" the girl inquired, in some alarm.

"Not at all," Mrs. V answered, "but in spite of that he has been here—he came and stood by my bed—'Mrs. V,' he said, 'I have come to bid you good-bye, and to ask for a lock of your hair to take with me.' I was not at all frightened. 'Henry,' I answered, 'how could you take a lock of my hair into the grave with you?' He smiled: 'it is only my body that will be in the grave,' he said: 'but I want you always to be sure that I came to you—that this was not a dream—so I will take a larger piece of hair than you would willingly give me.' He put his finger on my head and marked a large space on the right side. 'In two days you will not have a hair there,' he said, 'and now I want you to do some things for me'—so and so—mentioning the name of his fellow boarder—'has stolen my watch; he has pawned it, and carries the ticket about his person.

'In my wardrobe closet is a little trunk full of clothing; you will find the key of the trunk in the pocket of my gray vest.

'Unlock it, and, hidden beneath everything else, you will find a pocket-book. In one side are memoranda of debts I owe; in the other, of sums of money that are owed to me. If some one will collect the latter, the former may be paid with the amount and the price the watch will bring.' He then went on to assure me that he was not as bad as people thought him, and did not mean to become a thief, etc., etc.—after which he laid his hand upon my head again, and went away."

The daughter listened as most daughters would, without believing. But she did not try to convince her mother that she had had a dream, for her fears pointed to delirium. The doctor's verdict, however, was that nothing of the sort was to be apprehended, and when, the next day, the hair fell from Mrs. V's head, in precisely the spot which she declared the ghostly finger had outlined, the family at last began to believe that Henry G—— had visited their mother, and the eldest son began to investigate the other matters. Taking authority into his own hands, he went to his friend's late residence—the funeral not yet having taken place—found that his watch *had* disappeared, and instantly interviewed the fellow boarder who had been indicated as having stolen the watch.

"I would like to have the ticket"—he said, without preface.

"What ticket?" the young man inquired.

"The pawn-ticket for Henry G's watch," V replied. The other put his hand into his vest pocket, and handed him a pawn-ticket. Young V then made search for the key, found it, discovered the trunk, of which he knew nothing, found it filled with such garments as had been spoken of in the vision, and in the bottom the pocket-book, in which the records described were arranged in the two different divisions spoken of. He then proceeded to collect the debts, dispose of the watch and apply the proceeds to the purpose which had been indicated in the vision.

Two or three times, while this was being done, Mrs. V averred that Henry, apparently the same as in life, came to her bed-side, and stood there, simply looking at her, calmly and pleasantly. I believe he did not speak again. The spot whence the hair had fallen remained bald for some time, but was at last covered.

This tale was told me in perfect good faith and I know all the members of the V family well. They are averse to being considered superstitious, and I was obliged to promise to withhold their names if I used this story.

The daughter who gave me the particulars, also told me that once, upon a time—her mother being absent in Europe—she dreamed she saw her ill and seated in a chair, with a large quilt folded over her knees, an elderly woman in attendance upon her, and heard her say:

"Ah! if my child were here, she would know just what to do for me."

Writing to her mother, she mentioned this dream; but a letter from the latter lady crossed her own, in which appeared these words: "I have been very ill, indeed, and Bridget (mentioning a person the daughter had never seen) did her best. But how I wanted you. The other day, as I sat shivering before the fire, with a quilt spread over my knees to warm them, I said to her—'ah! if my child were here, she would know just what to do for me.'"

The words were the same Miss V had heard in her dream.

The mother said "my child," not "my daughter,"

which would have seemed more natural, as Miss V was the only girl in the family of brothers, and had attained the years of womanhood. So it was in the dream.

Again, this young lady dreamed, one night, that on that day, at a certain hour, her father's mother departed this life.

A memorandum of the hour was made, and the fact was that the death, which was not expected, had occurred at the precise time indicated in the dream.

EXTRACT FROM A LETTER.

JAN. —— 94.

"Don't you want a bit of occult news? At least, I want to tell you what happened to me on my way from St. Louis, going south-west.

"I do not know just where we were; but it was in the early morning—every one in good spirits, lots of talk, none of the dullness usual to car journeys. The weather was the cause, I suppose—bright, after a long spell of rain—but, certainly, the gayety of the passengers was markedly noticeable.

"Only one person in our car seemed 'out of it.' This was a man who lay with his head back, his eyes half open and his hands dropped on the cushions.

"As time passed, I heard one or two people exchange remarks about him. A lady said that he looked as if he were very ill. A man, *of course*, declared that he was intoxicated, and a girl giggled to another 'he's putting it on—thinks we'll admire him in that attitude.'

"I, myself, thought I would keep an eye on him, for

it looked to me as though he were in a very strange condition.

"Suddenly, however, without a word of warning, he started up, caught the rope that connects with the engineer's bell and snapped it, evidently giving the proper signal, for the train began to slow up, and stopped.

"Those in our car who knew that the man had rung the bell, began to cry out: 'what is the matter?'—'why did you do that?' and some to swear at him, or call him 'drunk' or 'crazy.'

"Excitement ran through the train, for the cars had stopped very suddenly and shaken people up, and the conductor, coming to make inquiry, inquired of the man—'come, now; don't you think you are a little too old to play tricks of this sort?'

"The stranger, however, standing pale and grave before him, sternly answered—'man, I stopped the train because we were rushing on to death. Send a party around the curve and you'll find the bridge down—I saw it down.'

"His tone impressed some of his traveling companions, and just then two gentlemen came in from the smoker, who seemed to be his friends. They began to insist on an investigation, and the feeling spread through the car.

"'Warnings have been given,' said one old man, who looked like a farmer; 'I guess it is so this time.'

"Consequently, many of the passengers followed the trainmen who were sent to see into the matter, and, having turned a curve that the train would have rounded in less than one minute, found, just beyond it, a chasm between two precipices, which had been spanned by a bridge. The bridge, however, was now down, and at the speed at which the train was going, it must have rushed into it with the usual frightful results.

"And, now, every one desired to thank the man they had abused and laughed at. But it seemed that he had gone off into a swoon, and his friends would not allow him to be disturbed. In fact, the bridge had been repaired and we were off again before he seemed to be himself—and then would or could offer no explanation, saying only:

"'I knew it, somehow; I saw it. Of course, I had the train stopped—that's all there is to it.'

A. W."

CHAPTER 15.

THE ANXIOUS MOTHER.

[As narrated to me by Fraulein Christine Hillern.]

In Frankfort dwelt, until recently, the lady whose story I shall now repeat. Her name was Christine Hillern, and she lived at home with her parents.

She was a very pleasing girl in every way, and, by nature, conscientious to the last degree. Her good qualities are plainly stamped upon her features and shine forth from her brilliant hazel eyes. She was, moreover, very religious, and constant in her attendance at church—she was a Lutheran.

As she sat, each Sunday, in her father's pew, she had, for many months, remarked the peculiar and earnest gaze which a lady, who occupied a place not far from her's, continually fixed upon her.

This lady she knew to be a Mrs. Jehn, wife of a respectable merchant of the place. She was invariably escorted by her husband, and a little boy and two little girls followed her up the aisle.

The gaze was gentle, kindly and almost loving, but its persistence was embarrassing. It seemed as if Mrs. Jehn was unable to remove her eyes from Christine's face, and, at last, one Sunday, as they came together in the church aisle, the matron touched the young lady on the arm and begged her to ask her mother's permission to call on her on a day and at an hour which she named. The young lady promised that she would, and Mrs. Jehn returned to her husband's side.

Christine, for her part, began to feel a great attraction toward this matron, so many years her senior, and Mrs. Hillern, willingly permitting her daughter to accept the invitation, for the Jehn's were known to be people of the best position. She began to be anxious for the period of her visit to arrive.

On the chosen day, having taken some pains with her toilette, and feeling pleased to think that she looked her best, Christine proceeded to the residence of the Jehn's and was ushered into the ladies' presence. Courtesies were exchanged, coffee and cakes were offered, the matron made many complimentary remarks, and, without flattering the young girl coarsely, showed an appreciation of her character and appearance that could not fail to be pleasing to the listener—since she seemed to know not only all she accomplished, but all she strove to be—to have an inner knowledge of her aspirations which amounted to mind-reading.

Before the guest took her leave, the hostess asked one question; it was this:

"Will you tell me, Miss Christine Hillern, whether you are betrothed, or whether your parents have their minds set upon your marriage with any one in particular?"

To this Christine replied, frankly, that she was entirely free; that she knew of no one she could possibly like well enough to marry, and that she felt that she would prefer a single life to any other. The lady smiled.

"At least, you have not chosen a husband," she said; "we will stop there. Surely, when a good man offers himself, you will think better of your idea of being a spinster."

She then kissed Christine, and begged her to come again in three days' time, and on no account to disappoint her.

Miss Hillern assented, and kept her promise. This time, after the coffee had been handed, the hostess begged her to come with her to her bedroom, and, locking the door, sat down beside her and took her hand. Her face was very sad and tears stood in her eyes.

"Miss Hillern," she said, "I am about to startle you very much—I am about to propose an alliance to you.

"The man is rich—I think him handsome—he is one who leads an upright life and who will be attentive to you. Would you feel averse to becoming the wife of a widower with three children?"

Miss Hillern, too much astonished to reply, could only look at Mrs. Jehn, who went on:

"You have seen the gentleman—he is my husband."

For a moment the young lady fancied that her new friend was insane; but she went on more calmly:

"Miss Christine, you see before you a dying woman —I may lie in this room, in my coffin, within three days. To-morrow an operation will be performed, under which I may die. If successful, I shall probably live a year and a half. I cannot expect a longer life than that, but I do pray, earnestly, to be left to my children so long. When I am gone, I wish my husband to marry as soon as public opinion will permit. The children must have a good mother—I have watched you carefully—I know you will be all to them that any one but myself can be, and I have selected you. Mr. Jehn admires you, and I have told him what I wish—in fact, if you assent, it is accomplished. Will you give me your promise to do as I wish?"

On this, a sort of horror filled the girl's soul, and she cried out to Mrs. Jehn to stop.

"Do you know what you say?" she exclaimed. "You are speaking to me of another woman's husband as a future lover. It is horrible! indecent! You may live after all! how can you?"

Mrs. Jehn began to weep violently.

"I have no sister," she sobbed, "no mother, no female relative. I shall be obliged to leave the world, knowing that my little ones will be ill-used by a cruel step-mother. Oh! the peace you would give me, were you to promise to care for my little ones.

"I shall not even be able to go to Heaven—I shall be earth-bound—obliged to witness their sufferings without being able to help them."

Finally, she grew so ill that Miss Hillern was alarmed, and, at last, she said—"I will never marry Mr. Jehn; but I will promise you that if you die, I will do all that your own sister would for the children—watch over them, see that they are properly taught and cared for, and that their moral and religious duties are not neglected."

Finally, Mrs. Jehn grew calm and thanked her.

A very painful and dangerous operation actually *was* performed next day. Mrs. Jehn survived it, and, to a stranger, seemed afterward to be in perfect health. But the doctor's verdict was unchanged. From that moment, Christine Hillern, with the devotion of a Sister of Charity, assisted her friend in the care of her children, learned her views and methods and won their love. The mother lingered somewhat longer than the period indicated by the doctors; but, before two years had gone, she had passed away.

Meanwhile, an indescribably perfect friendship had grown up between Miss Hillern and herself, and they read each other's very hearts. No one was surprised when one, so intimate with the household, still devoted herself to the interests of the three motherless children, and "Aunt Christine" was the being on whom the little ones depended most for love and consolation.

The widower grieved sincerely; but, one day, he made an offer to Christine, who declined it. In the course of a few years he offered himself three times, and seemed to have fallen seriously in love with Miss Hillern.

This made it rather unpleasant for her to perform her duties to the little ones; but she continued them until the widower put an end to the possibility of doing so, by marrying another woman.

The new wife frowned upon Mrs. Jehn's old friend, and played the traditional role of the step-mother to the full extent.

Finally, the family removed to America, and, though Miss Hillern still wrote to the boy "Albert" for some time, the step-mother soon intercepted the letters, found in those of her husband's son complaints of her cruel usage and the unhappiness of his home, and put a stop to the correspondence.

Now comes in the ghostly portion of the narrative, as related by Miss Hillern.

Some years had passed by. One Sabbath evening, Miss Hillern sat at the open window of her bedroom. The night was deliciously sweet and bright, and she had lit no lamp.

She was in a mood for reverie, and her thoughts were of her dead friend, Mrs. Jehn, and with the children, whom she so dearly loved. She could not wish that she had married the widower; but, she said to herself, that if she had been able to overcome her repugnance to such a step, Albert, Hedwig and Annie would surely have been happier. She could have been a true mother to them, for her whole heart was theirs. Then she said to herself that Albert was now a young man, and perhaps able to care for his sisters. She hoped he had done so.

It was at this moment that an impression was made upon her mind, which it is impossible to put into words. It was as though a mere veil interposed between herself and some scene of dissipation—what was to her appreciation a hideous orgy.

With it came the thought of Albert.

The impression was brief, but terrible—what it meant she could not comprehend—it left her quite unnerved and very sorrowful.

As she leaned back, with closed eyes, her thoughts still bent on Albert, she heard a soft, rustling sound—to use her own words: "as of a very light and graceful person, clothed in a robe of gossamer, who could walk without a footfall. Such a person was not to be found within the house, so I kept my eyes closed—when, closer to me, I once more heard the soft sounds, and, looking up, saw a tall, slender figure gliding into my room. It wore a floating robe of great length and fullness, no more substantial than tulle. It passed near me, floated away again, returned and seated itself opposite me, and I recognized my dead friend, Mrs. Jehn. I desired to greet her, but felt that if I spoke she would vanish. She seemed to understand me without words, but at last she spoke to me.

"'Where is Albert?' she asked, in a voice of indescribable sweetness, so soft and low, not like any human voice.

"Again I tried to impress upon her my grief that I did not know. Then her face assumed the expression it had worn when she told me she must die and leave her children. She sat there in silence for awhile—my eyes never left her face. Finally, she vanished."

Miss Hillern then went on to tell me that in a few days she received a letter from Albert. He wrote that, as he sat by the window of his room on that same Sunday night, thoughts of his dear, departed mother came to him. Her image arose before him so vividly that he could almost imagine her present, and with it came a thought of Miss Hillern, "Aunt Christine," as he called her, and he sent her his address, hoping for one of the "old, kind, affectionate letters."

Miss Hillern, in this way, learned the young man's

whereabouts, and so impressed was she by what she firmly believes to have been the visit of her friend's spirit, that she had the courage to write as a mother would to a son who had plunged into a vortex of dissipation.

His reply proved that this was so, and she told him what she had seen on that Sunday evening.

"Your mother cannot rest in Heaven until she knows that you will meet her there," she said, and the boy, greatly impressed, and deeply moved, promised reformation, and kept his word.

He is now an exemplary citizen, happily married, and able to shelter his sisters under his own roof.

"It is a proof," Miss Hillern says, "that a mother will even leave her home in the city beyond the skies for the sake of her children."

Of each mortal's own nature is born his occult experiences, colored by individual habit of thought and belief. Only a woman like Miss Christine Hillern would so have interpreted the motive of the ghostly visitant. But this gives us no reason for doubting the tale.

I have an idea that the Freed Spirit and the spirit still resident in the mortal frame are both needed to complete a vision of any importance.

Who can read the works of Emanuel Swedenborg, and dare to call him either madman or liar? But we all know that no plain, uneducated Methodist would have had such visions as his.

It might have been given the good man to have his spiritual sight opened, but he would not have seen the same sort of thing at all.

We make our own spiritual experiences here—so it may be through eternity.

To Miss Hillern came the charge to lead a stray lamb into the fold. To others, a simple "I love you"; "I wait for you—we will meet again," suffices. Again, there are people who only receive these visitations in the interests of real estate and portable property.

When an old gentleman, who has outlived all his dear ones, believes that he sees their forms beside him, or even that he can communicate with them by feeing trance-mediums and slate-writers, the lawyers find this an excellent reason for assisting his second cousins to take away his property and shut him up in a "retreat." But, curiously enough, there are many well-authenticated stories of lawyers, lawyers' clerks, and even judges, who have dreamed dreams in which the whereabouts of valuable documents have been revealed, and who have seen the spirits of departed clients at their bedsides at the dead of night: Spirits who have come to tell them where to find a missing will—and who have condescended to search in the places indicated by the vision, with most satisfactory results.

The average legal mind can act in unison with a spirit who returns to earth for such a purpose, and is not in the least ashamed of having such a vision. Nor have I ever heard of a lawyer believing himself unable to manage other people's affairs because of an hallucination of this sort.

It is the Italian, ready for the vendetta, or the Frenchman who is a practiced duelist, to whom the form of his friend appears, touching the wounds in his breast, whispering, "avenge me."

Spirits at least know how to put the right man in the right place.

The devout Catholic is requested in his dream, or vision, to have masses said for the soul that cannot rest until this has been done. Who ever heard of a departed spirit going to a Quaker for this object, even to a Protestant?—though they have visited the latter frequently, in order to have their bodies properly buried, with a neat tombstone overhead, instead of lying doubled up under the cellar stairs.

Those who had an interest in funerals, while living, no doubt felt some in the other state—at least for a time.

"The ruling passion, strong in death," may be strong after it.

A hundred odd years ago, a gay Lothario, who had "wronged a maid" and driven her to suicide, was sure to see her reproachful ghost. I have no doubt that he did ; certainly he deserved to do so.

TWO PICTURES OF HEAVEN.

Preachers understand, or should, that the same spiritual appeal will not move all men.

The man who wishes to thrill his audience will be careful to discover to what manner of people he is speaking before he opens his lips. To some he talks of a Heaven where love abides and we shall see our dear ones. To others of palaces and gardens of roses —such as never bloom on earth.

I had, one Sunday morning, heard something beautiful of this sort from one who had a wonderful command of language, and who described the Heaven of his hopes and dreams in a magnificent church, with painted windows and cushioned pews. His congregation was made up of people who were daily surrounded by beautiful objects, who had most of them traveled and seen all that the world has of the lovely and marvelous. It was necessary to make his Heaven very, very wonderful, exquisitely lovely, to fire their imaginations; but he did it. Poets listened; artists saw the picture before them; tender-hearted women wept; sensuous eyes sparkled. The man did what he pleased with his listeners, and the best of it was, it all came from his heart—to him Heaven was like that, probably will be. It was rather oriental, and I think my Heaven will be a little plainer, with a quiet corner in it here and there, and more moonlight. But it was exceedingly beautiful. I went, that very afternoon, to hear some preaching in a tent. It was a woman who spoke that day, a large, broad-shouldered person, neither well-educated nor well-informed. She was not always grammatical; but all the better for that could she bring herself *en rapport* with her audience—principally hardworking women, in shabby gowns and cheap hats, washerwomen, janitresses, who had to stretch their sinfully small wages to cover bread and meat, fire and rent for a large family of small children, and helpless old people. But they were self-respecting folk for all that, as people who go to church usually are.

The preacher, who stood on the platform, dressed in

black silk and a widow's cap, with a voice that filled every corner of the great tent, pleased them well. Sometimes she made them wipe away a tear or two; sometimes they hid smiles behind their handkerchiefs, when she said "such true things" about men staying away from church or scolding over late dinner, and at last she began to talk of Heaven.

"Why, sisters!" she shouted, "I shall go before some of you, that is certain, and when you get there I want you to come and see me—right off—come and take tea. I mean to build my house at the corner of Glory street and Hallelujah avenue; anybody will show you the way. Walk right in; the door will always be open—wide open, sisters, everybody welcome, enough to eat and drink for all. I shall expect you; we'll all be there, sisters, glory!" For one moment I laughed; then I was disgusted. Then I looked at the faces about me, and saw so many radiant with hope, covered with smiles, that my mood changed. The preacher had drawn a picture of Heaven that seemed very beautiful to these tired souls. No more washing, no more scrubbing, no more counting of pennies—a perpetual state of holiday tea-drinking. And then they would all be there: lost mothers and fathers; John, who came courting so long ago; the baby, who pined away and withered in the cradle—they realized it all, and joined in the shout of "glory." And when the singing band began the hymn—"There's a Mansion in Heaven for Me"—everybody sang, and there was no one to tell them they made discords, or that a lovelier picture might be drawn of Paradise than their cheerful, loud-voiced

preacher in the widow's cap had placed before them.
They would no more have comprehended the morning's sermon than they could have understood Wagner's music, or admired the greatest masterpiece of the greatest painter. They had their congregational singing, and liked the chromo of "the Little Girl with the Kitten"—on the walls at home—the one given with their pound of tea, for the sentiments conveyed, not for art's sake. And their Heaven had no art in it, either, only peace and re-union of dear ones. The rest they would, one day, learn.

THE CASE OF MRS. ROGER BLACK.

A Mr. Roger Black, a plain man, living in Kentucky, had just paid for a small house, which he had hitherto rented, and, returning home, told his wife, showed her the receipt for the sum—two thousand dollars—though more regular papers were to be made out next day, and, as far as she knew, he then went at once to his stable, where, some hours later, he was found dead, having been kicked in the head by a horse.

When the first horror was over, and Mr. Black's funeral had taken place, the widow naturally looked for the receipt, but could not find it. Having incautiously mentioned this fact, the person who had sold the property denied having received any money from Mr. Black, and insinuated that Mrs. Black uttered a falsehood when she declared that her husband had done more than talk about buying the place. In proof of this, he showed a document, only half completed, and declared that Black had said: "let it wait until I think it over"—and that, for his part, he had been very willing to wait.

The widow naturally fought for her rights, but had no case.

She had no witnesses, and the lawyer who had the interests of the other side in charge brought witnesses to prove that Mrs. Black was the victim of hallucinations—thought that her mother's spirit sat at her bedside when she was ill, and had held spiritual circles at her house. Believing in an alleged medium, who was afterward exposed, and in warnings of Mr. Black's death, in the shape of raps on her head-board.

People who could not believe Mrs. Black capable of trying to defraud anyone, readily leaned to the idea that she was the victim of delusion, and the poor woman, who could not prove the truth of her statement to anyone, was also aggrieved by being supposed insane.

The night before the decision took place, she gave up all hope and went early to bed, taking her two little ones with her.

She could not sleep, but lay there weeping, wondering how she could feed her children, from whom their hard-earned home was to be wrested. There was a public clock not far away, and she heard it strike, nine—ten—eleven—at last twelve—then, weary with her sorrowful vigil, her eyes closed.

She lay in a deep and heavy slumber, when she was aroused by heavy blows upon her outer door. As she was alone in the little house, she felt alarmed, and, pushing up the window, leaned out and asked who was there.

To her surprise, the voice of the lawyer who was working against her replied:

"It is I—come down, Mrs. Black; I must speak to you."

Accordingly, she dressed and went to the door. In the cold, gray dawn, they stood there together, and she saw that something moved him strongly.

"Mrs. Black," he said, at last, "to-night, as I lay in bed, I thought that your late husband came into my room, and stood looking at me. I do not believe in such things as apparitions, you know; but I could not fancy it a delusion when he spoke—'you are helping that man to rob my wife,' he said; 'I did pay him the money. We were to have a lawyer make out papers next day. I showed wife the receipt and then put it in my mother's old bureau, up garret, where I keep other papers, in the secret drawer—get it.'

"Then," said the lawyer, "a light by which I saw him, faded—I got up and came to you." The widow shook her head—"I am afraid *you* have been having hallucinations now," she said; "poor Roger never would have put the receipt there. To be sure, there is a secret drawer—I will go and see—come up."

She led the way up to the garret, in the corner of which stood a broken, old bureau. There was a so-called secret drawer between two manifest ones. She touched the spring—a number of yellow papers lay there and some Daguerreotypes. Amongst them was a large, white envelope.

"That is it!" Mrs. Black cried, drew it forth, opened it, and—behold! the receipt.

"Mrs. Black, you have but to bring that receipt to court to-morrow," the lawyer said, slowly; "my client is a rascal.

"If I may ask you a favor—it is this—that you will keep the secret of my vision, it would greatly injure me to have it known. But I do not think that you are anxious for revenge?"

Mrs. Black held out her hand to him.

"You have done me a good turn by coming here," she said, "and I promise."

"I wonder my poor husband went to you—I should have thought he'd come to me instead—but you acted right, and I'll never tell."

She never did, while the lawyer lived. After he died, she no longer felt bound by the promise she had made him.

I do not vouch for this story. It was told me as a true one; but it resembles very closely a tale in an English periodical many years old. However, it is an illustration of my idea that lawyers are employed by spirits who have legal affairs to settle before they can forget the troubles of this world.

CHAPTER 16.

THE MEDIUMS OF UNCIVILIZED NATIONS.

Under various names that which the modern Spiritualist calls "a medium" is to be found in nearly every savage nation upon the face of the globe. There are but few of these people who do not believe that man's soul is immortal, and who do not profess to believe that their departed friends still take an interest in the affairs of those they have left behind them.

One of the greatest difficulties the missionaries have had in converting many of these people, lies in the impossibility of making them willing to think that their souls will rest until the Judgment-day, and then depart for all eternity to Heaven or hell. Neither does the idea of purgatory meet their views. They insist upon the ability of the spirit to come and go at will. They usually accord it a residence much more delightful than this world can be, and are very ready to believe in Heaven, especially one of what someone calls "the jewelers' show-window sort"—all diamonds and rubies, and gold and pearls—but the doors of this place are always ajar; they will not have the Freed Spirit locked in, even there.

"Mus *come*," said an African savage to a missionary, "mus *see*, fader, moder, wife, brudder, if lub."

Surely, his soul must have comprehended the fact

that, whatever our spirits keep or lose, their affections remain to them. If we love much, absence is unendurable.

THE KAFFIRS.

As to what savages believe, it is often hard to be sure—they are very reticent; but most of them have some notion of a creator. The Kaffirs call him by a word which signifies "Great Great." They say that Great Great, having created the world and lived here until the green things grew, took a seed and split it, and from one half came man, from the other woman; into them he breathed the immortal spirit, and gave them the world for their own.

When the body dies, the soul goes down, and it becomes its mission to advise its friends for their best good.

If living folk forget lost friends, the spirits grieve and are apt to recall themselves to mind by some slight punishment.

By way of reparation, the relatives sacrifice cattle to the dead. They make a feast—the living eat the meat. The spirits of the animals join those in the spirit herds, of which the ghosts are just as fond as they were of those they owned in life, and there is a family reconciliation.

THE ASHANTEES.

Ashantees believe in a creator and in hosts of evil spirits. Their belief as to the soul of a man is that it returns to a human body. They call the soul the "kra." It is a sort of spiritual Siamese twin—one half good, and the other half evil. When a little baby dies, its soul, they say, enters the form of the next child borne by its mother, who considers it the same individual and hails its return with joy. In fact, the strong point of their belief as to man's soul is eternal re-incarnation. Mediums are "controlled" by spirits which were never men or women, mostly for evil, but sometimes in order that they may make prophecies.

THE DAHOMIANS.

In Dahomey the mediums are called "Fetish-men." They are controlled as mediums are. A party of people appoint an hour for a seance—the fee is a silver dollar or its value.

The Fetish-man goes into a trance; his spirit visits the other world, and, on returning, he tells the news he has gathered.

If any one is ill, it is supposed to be because his departed friends are calling him. On this, the Fetish-man is consulted, and sent to the spirit-world to give the spirits reasons why they should let him remain on earth awhile longer—making polite excuses, but signifying that his work here is not yet done.

Sometimes they refuse to listen; but if they accord him a longer life, the Fetish-man assures the suppliants that their friend will recover, and, besides his fee, has a present of value.

The excuse sometimes is that the patient is not yet

rich or powerful enough, and it is considered a good one: for, as the people of Dahomey go into the next world, so they remain. A king is a king eternally, a servant a servant; if one goes over poor, he can never be rich.

Therefore, "we excuse him until he has (so many) cattle," is a reply often reported by the Fetish-man as being sent by the very spirits who are most anxious to have their friends "come down"—curiously it is *down*, not up.

THE AUSTRALIANS.

The medium of the Australians is called a "Charm Man."

Their spirit-home is up, for they always point to the sky.

There seems to be a sort of limbo, in which, when a man first dies, he wanders about in utter darkness. At last he finds a pendent rope or cord, seizes it, and is pulled up to his future dwelling, where he becomes white.

Therefore, spirits appear with white skins. There is but one word in the native language for ghost and European.

When white men and women were first seen, they were hailed as the spirits of the departed, and were "recognized" just as good Spiritualists recognize their friends at the doors of materializing mediums' cabinets—no very close resemblance was expected.

A Mrs. Thompson, a plain, Scotch widow, who (I

believe) was one of a party shipwrecked on Western Prince of Wales Island, fell under the notice of a certain chief, who instantly flew to the conclusion that she was the spirit of his lost daughter, "Griom," whom he had tenderly loved, and who had returned to him, solidly materialized. He welcomed her with joy and took her home.

Not understanding the Scottish tongue, he was not aware that she denied the fact, and insisted on being a good father to her. She was unutterably wretched, but he never knew it.

Finally, she learned to talk a little, and the kind parent married her to what seemed to her a very frightful savage, but who was considered a most eligible match by Australians.

However, the women were always afraid of her, and would warn their children not to vex "the ghost."

When, at last, she contrived to make her position known to some English sailors, and received the protection of the captain and officers, many efforts were made to induce her to remain, and the old chief, who believed her his daughter, lamented her as he would have done were she dying.

Nor was this a solitary instance where white people were taken to the hearts of Australians as the spirits of dead friends and relatives.

Some departed souls are supposed to enter animals— the Charm Men know these at sight—and their lives are saved.

The Australian has no name for God—but they speak of a First Man, whose name was "Adi." He was alone on the earth with his wives, and, while fishing, was drowned.

His wives witnessed this catastrophe, and afterward saw a great, black rock start up where he had gone down. Thereupon they flung themselves into the sea, and so committed suicide, and came up again, as he did, in the shape of rocks. So there stands great, black Adi, its back far above the water, and about it a circle of little rocks, called the Spile, or the wives, who, in this way, still attend their husband.

Sometimes, through the Charm Men, the survivors of a family learn that the departed is unhappy. Peace can be secured to him, if one of their number will spend a dark night alone, lying upon his grave. The ordeal is terrible; but some are found devoted and affectionate enough to offer themselves. During this time, the unhappy spirit is supposed to appear to him, and he is put to indescribable torture of mind and body; but if he endures all bravely, not only does the spirit have peace, but he himself becomes endowed with occult powers, and is respected thereafter as a sorcerer.

The Australians believe in a river-spirit, like the German Necken, in a wood-demon, with horns and saucer eyes, ycleped "Bunyip," and in a great bird called the "Marralya," who appears beside the bedsides of sick people and squeezes out their breath with its great claws, or even tears them to pieces with its beak. Within this bird dwells no spirit of its own; but it is entered by those of witches who are enemies of the sick person.

The Maoris of New Zealand speak of a great spirit, "Atna"; of a bad spirit, "Wairua."

They pray and offer sacrifices of flesh, and also sacrifices of the fruits of the earth.

They never opposed Christian missionaries, but welcomed them from the first—mixing the faith to which they were supposed to be converted, with much that was foreign to it and shocking to the missionaries.

When man's spirit departs, they say, it goes to "Reinga," which seems to be a sort of Heaven. They believe shooting-stars to be spirits on their way to Reinga. They seem to have no doubt that spirits can converse with and counsel their living friends, but this only in the presence of a medium, for whom their name is "Tohunga." He is usually clairaudient, and interprets what spirits say to the anxious friends who sit about him.

They only hear a faint whistling, like a gentle breeze. Sometimes he sees a pale light, or the shadow of a form, and considers it the spirit; but even to him it is always faint and vague.

There is a sort of Maori Charon, who manages a canoe with sail and paddles, and takes the Free Spirit across the waters between life and death. Sometimes, mourning relatives provide the deceased with a boat of this sort, which they place upon his grave. It is too small for real navigation—a sort of model, in fact, but well provided with stores of food and water for the voyage.

They believe in evil spirits, and hear their voices in the air, and are so much afraid of witches, that any old woman, who can make them believe that she is one, can have things all her own way. The witches are said to dig a hole in the ground at midnight, utter a spell, and invoke the spirit of the person she desires to injure, which appears like a flame, is cursed, and carries home the curse to the sleeping body.

However, people pray for the sick—much as pious folk do in this country—addressing Atna, the Great Spirit, only.

For a long time, the gigantic and grotesque figures on the coast were called idols; but it is now known that they never worshipped them.

THE FIJIANS.

Priests are the mediums of the Fijians. As one explained it to a white man, his state, when entranced, is this:

"My own mind departs. When it is truly gone, and I, myself, know nothing, my God speaks within me."

To begin his seance, the priest anoints and adorns himself, and on the arrival of the person who wishes to consult him, sits with his back toward the large, white cloth, which is always suspended behind him on such occasions, and has near him a bowl of perfumed oil.

The visitors enter, present the priest with certain offerings, amongst them a whale's tooth, and tell him their motive in consulting him.

Having heard all they have to say, the priest takes the tooth into his hand and fixes his eyes upon it—all sit in a circle about him and are utterly silent, closely watching him.

Soon he shivers, trembles, his face is distorted, the blood-vessels stand out like ropes, his heart is almost seen to beat.

Then he grows pale and seems to shrivel—his expression becomes that of a furious madman; he weeps, perspires profusely, and what he calls his "god" is supposed to have possession of him, and communications begin. At last, a voice utters:

"I depart." The priest throws himself on the ground, and his "god" returns to the world of spirits.

Sometimes the priest holds his seance at the private house of an important person—the white cloth, however, is always necessary.

THE ABYSSINIANS.

The Abyssinians are, many of them, supposed to be Christians. They pray and fast—particularly fast—but they believe in many things that their pastors and masters hold in abhorrence.

Their greatest horror is a "Bouda," and their belief that one can transform any man into a dog, a donkey, or any beast of the field, keeps them in perpetual anxiety.

He, himself, usually takes the shape of a hyena, and is then heard laughing in the forests.

A medium, with them, is the wretched victim of sorcery, who, for the time, speaks and moves at the bidding of the evil spirit put into his body, or frequently, her body.

An Englishman, who, with a party of conscientious

companions, was witness to one of these supposed "obsessions" or "possessions," has minutely described it:

The medium was a girl. For days she had been moving listlessly about, complaining of her head—then she became entranced, and lay motionless. Her friends said that the Bouda had entered her, and watched her in sorrow and alarm. An English physician was allowed to do what he pleased to arouse her; in vain. She lay motionless, and a voice seemed to proceed from her, without the use of her teeth, or tongue, or throat.

At last, suspecting deception, the physician applied strong liquid ammonia to the girl's nostrils. It was a fluid unknown to any there; but, though she had no experience of *sal-volatile*, the Abyssinian damsel never winced. Cold water, thrown upon her in a sudden douche, produced no gasp.

The friends lamented and carefully guarded the door of the hut.

"Soon," they said, "Bouda will make her try to go to the hyena. He will howl in a few moments." And, curiously enough, it was not long before the hideous, laughing cry of the creature resounded from the forest, where it had not been heard for days.

The physician and his friends remained in the hut all night.

After awhile, the girl spoke gently and seemed in her right mind. She asked if she might go out and breathe the fresh air, saying that she was now quite well, and, arising, walked toward the door, like an animal, as we say, "on all fours." But her relatives, crying out that this was only the Bouda trying to get her outside of the hut by artifice, seized her gently and kindly, bound her hands and feet together, tied her up in such a fashion that it must have taken many moments to unbind the cords, laid her on a mat and covered her with something.

Instantly she arose—every knot untied—and walked toward the door in the same fashion.

It was no exhibition, nothing was to be gained by it; but again and again the girl was bound, the Englishman assisting in securing the knots, and she regularly threw off the cords the moment she had been laid upon the mat again.

This was repeated again and again, until a fearful howl filled the hut. The girl opened her eyes, swooned away, and the Bouda was said to have departed. Whereupon the relatives expressed their satisfaction in their sister's recovery.

SPIRITUAL BELIEF OF THE ESQUIMAUX.

Persons who have taken the trouble to converse with the Esquimaux as to their spiritual faith, have made many curious discoveries.

They believe in a supreme being and a holy mother, in the immortality of the soul and two future states, one of reward and one of punishment. The latter is described as a place where snow falls perpetually and a storm of sleet never ceases. Through these, blinded and benumbed, the unhappy hunter pursues a seal which is merely a phantom and never can be caught.

He is hungry; he longs for his friends and his home: but can never eat, or rest, or be comforted. Could imagination create a more wretched hell?

However, this is only for the very worst. Their crimes are so few that it is hard to think this frozen Hades very thickly populated. Esquimaux do not fight or commit murder, or even make war. Such social laws as they have are never infringed. They are honest to a degree. A knife is the most precious possession of an Esquimau, a sharp tool of any sort a temptation; but anyone can drop such things anywhere and be sure of finding them just where he left them. The hunters of phantom seals, perhaps, have "made bad Karma"; have *thought* evil things, not done them.

But the good Esquimau, when he dies, enjoys himself. He can visit his friends at will, and finds in his spirit-home nearly the same pleasures he would have experienced here if there had been neither sickness or death—he is always young and happy.

People have called the Esquimaux unfeeling, because they do not pay any regard to a dead body and leave people to die alone.

This latter custom, however, arises from a belief that, at the moment of the spirit's departure, a band of immortal beings gather about him, and that mortals are in the way. Therefore, they build him a new hut, light a lamp, and leave him to angelic ministrations.

As to the body, an Esquimau explained that in this fashion: "If my friend threw away the body, like old clothes not wanted, now he has new, why should I care for? The body is nothing."

Yet, an Esquimau often sits by a grave, talking to spirits very earnestly.

"Do they answer you?" was asked of one who did this for a long while.

"Yes, within me," said the Esquimau, tapping his breast softly—"not so"—and he touched his ears.

Some Esquimaux also profess to see spirits. Usually not those of departed friends, but queer, tricky sprites, resembling Robin Goodfellow, who torment the maids and men, much as he did those of old England. These creatures, who are described as having very ugly faces—though, who can say what may seem ugly in the eyes of an Esquimau?—are supposed to sit and grin at mortals in such hideous fashion that there is no bearing it.

They put out the lamps by blowing at them, disturb the wet clothes in the "dry net," so that they dry unevenly, and jog the elbows of the women as they sit carving ivory, which is one of their favorite occupations, and in which they show great skill. Moreover, they make the babies cry, break the children's toys, and tangle the "cat's cradle," which is one of their games.

A loud and peculiar shriek, made with the fingers in the mouth, is the only method of exorcising these household demons.

A man will say to others:

"Excuse me, but a demon is troubling me—permit me to howl."

They believe, also, in sea spirits, who live beneath the water and keep "herds" of whales and walrus.

In their clairvoyance, the clairvoyant in his trance

visits the homes of powerful spirits and paints word-pictures of their residences as minute as Swedenborg's descriptions of his heavens. And they have their spirit-rappers. These are possessed by what they call a "Tornga," which is exactly what the medium of our country designates his "control."

The "seance" is always a dark one. The assemblage is seated, silence is enjoined, and (as far as the matter can be decided by the sense of hearing) the medium begins to throw himself about, to dance and whirl in circles. Certainly he howls, gabbles, hisses and invokes the Tornga.

Shortly, he sits down on the ground and is quiet; he holds his breath, so that those who have carefully examined him cannot detect the least respiration. While he lies thus, seemingly dead, loud slaps are heard, which announce the arrival of the Tornga. They are made on any solid body adapted to the purpose. Two slaps announce the arrival; questions are answered by other slaps, as in table-rappings.

At last, Tornga gives a final slap, to signify that he is going, gabbles, hisses and howls. His voice seems to die away in the distance, and the medium comes to life, with a howl, uttered without previous respiration.

No Esquimau has ever attempted to "investigate," or to "grab."

CHAPTER 17.

TESTIMONY FROM ALL QUARTERS.

There are many people who feel it their mission to prove to the world at large, that all apparitions, omens, and occult experiences whatsoever, are simply caused by disturbances of the brain, defects of the eye and ear, and freaks of the imagination.

Doubtless, many of these are so caused, and the knowledge of this fact is of use to the medical man, who generally needs all the help he can get in every direction. Also to nervous people, who are frightened when old furniture creaks, and take a rat in the surbase for "a warning," and a dream caused by mincepie and green-tea, swallowed at midnight, for a revelation from on high. I think, too, it is well to teach the maid who is afraid to go up-stairs in the dark, and the coachman who gives warning because the weather-vane on the barn needs oiling, and represents to his fancy a most wretched and unhappy ghost "groaning awful," that superstition is sinful. But people who deny the fact to prove that they have fine minds are really hindering progress.

The general dread of being thought superstitious is very much in the way of anything like Psychical research in respectable circles.

Thousands of stories of dreams, "warnings," clairvoyant-trances and the appearance of dead friends, are hidden away by respectable families, as if they were skeletons which would disgrace them if they peeped out of their closets.

Especially is this so in the Northern States of America.

English folk have no objection to being known to have, at their "place in the country," a white lady, or a mysterious figure in a cloak, or a chariot that drives to the gate and vanishes. In fact, they are apt to tell of it, for it is aristocratic. No German castle is without its spectre, no church without its legends, and it is the learned professor or the man of science who is most apt to take an interest in anything relating to "the debatable land."

Here, the wise are too anxious to be thought so. Those who follow my leader, wait for them to jump. It is so at the North, at all events. Most Southerners are more emotional and romantic, and ready to accept the fact that tokens of affectionate remembrance are sometimes sent to mortals from those who have gone before. Besides, people who have always been surrounded by negroes, must learn that much which is usually treated with scorn as absurd, is based on facts as strange and inexplicable as they are positive.

The slaves, descendants of savages, knew the power of a thought to harm—well for us, if we should recognize it. Most of us believe that we can treasure hate for an individual, if we conceal it within our bosoms and do not speak of it. If we use the object of our hate kindly, we really feel as though we merited the smiles of Heaven.

THE FREED SPIRIT. 203

It is hard to comprehend that an evil thought goes forth and does its work, and, moreover, like the boomerang, is apt to return at last, to the hand that sent it.

And in this let those take comfort who have made mistakes and done the very thing they should not have done, with good intentions, moved by love or friendship, or general feelings of humanity. The mistake will have its effect here—we must suffer for mistakes—but the good thought, the pure intention, will also fulfil its appointed task.

Having wandered away from my sheep, I return to them.

There are proper opinions to hold, for instance, in regard to the appearance of spirits—they must be spoken of as "hallucinations" by persons of good sense. The editor of a magazine of position must keep up its credit for being ably directed.

Therefore, when he mentions anything remarkable in the occult line, he must head it to suit the tastes of the general reader.

The general reader of a popular paper is supposed to be unable to comprehend anything beyond the reach of a child's intelligence. The general reader of the magazine is held to be respectable and conservative, and above all, to hold the regular stock opinion on all subjects. Therefore, one of the cleverest magazines in the country heads a column with these words:

"Hallucinations of the senses," and explains, carefully, that *he* knows that they are nothing more, and that he does not presume to imagine for a moment that any reader on his subscription list would entertain any other opinion, and then goes on to tell the following well-authenticated ghost stories:

"On the night of November 17, 1890, Mr. S. Walker Anderson, of Tickhill, Bawtry, Yorkshire, then in Australia, woke up in bed and distinctly saw the figure of his aunt, Mrs. Pickard, standing, with her arms down, near the foot of the bed, and dressed in an ordinary black dress, such as he had seen her wear many times. She looked older and stouter than when he had last seen her, three years before, and she moved her lips as if to say 'goodby,' and then vanished by degrees. There was a lamp in the room and he was wide awake. He had not been anxious about her; but, on seeing the vision, began to fear that she was dead, and took a note of the time, which was about midnight. The mail brought news of her death at 11:00 A. M., November 17.

"The Rev. Matthew Frost, of Bowers Gifford, Essex, states that on the first Thursday of April, 1887, while sitting at tea, with his back to the window, and talking to his wife, he plainly heard a rap on the window, and, looking around, saw his grandmother tapping on the glass, and said to his wife: 'Why, there's my grandmother,' and went to the door, and even round the house, for he felt sure his grandmother was about, but could see no one. On the following Saturday he received news that his grandmother, who lived in Yorkshire, died about half an hour before he heard the raps.

"Miss P——, mistress in a high school, was walking to the school on April 6, 1887, after eight o'clock in the morning, and distinctly saw her father. Three days before, she had a presentiment of coming trouble and could not stay alone. Two telegrams to the school announced her father's illness and death on April 6."

Now, if the editor really believed that these were hallucinations, and no more, why should he feel called upon to pay them any attention? If Mr. Anderson, the Rev. Matthew Frost and Miss P——, were, for a few moments, feverish or delirious, or had some trouble with their eyes—that was not a matter to interest the world at large, nor would he so have regarded it.

Like all other human beings, that editor seized the tiny bit of testimony that death is not annihilation, with avidity; but, being wise in his generation, he touched it up with a bit of practical good-sense before he sent it to the compositor.

Mr. Jones, of "Jones & Jingles," would, perhaps, have stopped his subscription, had the article been headed as it might have been, but "hallucinations of the senses" made it quite the correct thing. While he read it, he felt a little more certain that he should, one day, see his dear, old mother, who died when he was only a poor clerk, and that she would be, in a measure, like herself. Wings and a harp create a feeling of remoteness; but he said—"curious hallucination of a clergyman, my dear"—before he read it to his wife, and the good lady so accepted it. Really, after all, it is only a matter of ceremony. If only the magazines will all publish everybody's hallucinations, and make it a genteel and sensible thing to have hallucinations—"hallucination" will, in time, appear in the dictionaries defined thus—"a spirit—a visitant from the other world."

And it is not a step, but a very long stride, that has been taken when such things are printed under any heading in periodicals intended for the perusal of the respectable and wealthy.

There are notable exceptions to the usual alarmed reticence.

The whole nation knows that Abraham Lincoln was a devout believer in signs and omens, and had several visions during his lifetime, most of which have been mentioned in print.

He never said "keep that to yourself," in telling them, or "I would not have the public know that for the world."

Honest to the very soul, he had no more hesitation in admitting his belief on occult subjects than on national ones.

What he saw he spoke of as the simplest peasant might. It never entered his mind that some might consider him foolish or a lunatic because of his supernatural stories—nor did any one ever draw such a conclusion. That was impossible.

Prophetic dreams he certainly had—one, the night before his own assassination.

In Carpenter's "Six Months at the White House," we find this: "At the Cabinet meeting, held the morning of the assassination, General Grant was present, and, during a lull in the conversation, the President turned to him and asked if he had heard from General Sheridan. General Grant replied that he had not, but was in hourly expectation of doing so.

"'You will hear very soon,' said the President,

'and the news will be important. I had a dream last night—and, ever since the war began, I have inevitably had the same dream before any important military event occurred. It is in your line, too, Mr. Welles—the dream was that I saw a ship sailing very rapidly.'"

The President had also visions that prophesied his death.

Many great men of the past are said to have had the moment of their death foretold. Xenophon says that Cyrus dreamed of the exact moment of his death. Socrates dreamed that a white lady came to him and quoted a passage from Homer, which predicted his death. Judas Maccabeus thought that the spirit of the bishop of Milan appeared in a certain spot, which he saw in his dream, and, pointing to the ground, said: "Here and in this place." And on that very spot, the following morning, his enemy gained a victory over him. Cæsar's wife, Calphurnia, had a dream which foretold his death. Aristotle says that Eudemius thus saw the death of Alexander. Caracalla foretold his own assassination, which he saw in a dream. For generations the members of an English family named "Wotten" were celebrated for dreaming of their own deaths, of which they foretold the date and the circumstances. Sir Thomas Wotten also described a burglary committed in Oxford, of which he dreamed as he slept in Kent, and named the burglars.

Before George Villiers, Duke of Buckingham, was murdered, stabbed to the heart by a dagger in the hands of John Felton, a lieutenant in the army, who fancied himself unjustly treated in regard to promotion, the air seemed full of portents—the duke being on his way to Portsmouth, whence he was about to set sail, commanding an expedition for the relief of the Protestants at La Rochelle. An old Highland seer, being requested by a Scottish nobleman to foretell Villiers' future, which seemed to promise well, fell into the usual state of trance, and, waking from it, said: "The man will come to nought. I see him with a dagger plunged in his heart."

Parker, who had been an officer of the wardrobe to the duke's father, thrice declared that his old patron had come to him in the night, and told him to warn his son that he had secret enemies, and, on the third time, had drawn a dagger from his bosom and said: "This will end my son's life—and do you, my good Parker, prepare for death, for it is near you."

He told the duke of this, and he left home in a pensive and apprehensive mood in consequence. However, no idea whence the danger was to be expected was given, or it might have been avoided. A little later, the duke's sister, the Countess of Denbigh, dreamed that she was riding with him in a coach, when she heard shouts of joy in the street.

"Why do they huzza?" she asked.

"Because the duke is dying," was the answer. She looked at him, saw that it was so, and, uttering a shriek, awoke.

Much agitated, she began to tell her dream to one of her ladies, and had just finished, when the news of his assassination was brought to her. I believe he was stabbed while alighting from his coach. Parker also died almost immediately.

Great faith was placed in prophetic dreams by wise men of the past. Cicero tells of two friends who traveled together; but, being, one night, unable to find accommodation in one inn, the one who stayed where they first called dreamed that his friend came to him and besought his aid, saying that his landlord was murdering him. He awoke, rejoiced that it was nothing but a dream, and slept again. This time he thought he saw his friend once more, and that he reproached him for not coming to his aid, and cried, in piteous accents: "It is now too late, for he has slain me." On this, the dreamer became convinced that the other man was actually dead, and, rising in consternation, sought the house of the man who had entertained him, and found that he had actually murdered his guest for what money he had about him.

Fancy a writer mentioning all these instances and many more, and then setting coolly to work to prove that there was really nothing in them, by quoting from Rasselas: "All power of fancy over reason is a degree of insanity," and declaring that dreams are nothing but a species of delirium.

Very easy to say; but how did this explain the vision of the governor who, one night, saw in his room what appeared to be no other than the celebrated Harvey, who was then in Dover, but about to leave it. Startled by the unexpected call, his excellency begged to know what brought him there.

"I am not exactly Harvey," said the presence, "but I am his spirit. He is at his house, in bed. He is determined to set sail for Calais to-morrow; but the packet that he intends to take will be lost. As we have still much work to do in this world, I come to ask you to detain him in Dover for four and twenty hours."

The governor pondered the matter over the rest of the night, and the next morning sent an order commanding Harvey to remain in Dover for a day or two. Naturally, that gentleman's astonishment was very great; but, as a storm arose, and the packet was lost, with most of her passengers, his wrath was turned to gratitude, and, subsequently the governor told him why he detained him. But for the disaster he would have kept his reasons to himself.

However, dreams are seldom of such real practical value. Usually, they do not point out the way of escaping danger, but only prophesy that it is at hand.

Most people, whose names we know, who have done great things in this world, think a good deal of what is to follow the present state. What interests them is not the sort of thing we "cannot take with us," but just the very reverse—what *may* go with the soul if our souls go anywhere, be part of our identity if we retain it.

CHAPTER 18.

THE BELIEF OF AGASSIZ IN THE ETERNAL CONTINUANCE OF INDIVIDUAL PERSONALITY.

Agassiz, despite his opposition to Spiritualism, believed that individual personality was retained in the future existence. Death, he said, might alter his mode of activity, but he should still be active, and that probably his soul would take delight in observing the souls of animals, as he now did their bodies.

One says of him: "His theory that animals have souls was derived from his intense knowledge of their nature."

Those who knew him say that he could talk to all so-called dumb creatures—that they hailed him with friendly cries and movements of the head, and loved him better than those who were always with them after they had seen him but once.

IMMANUEL KANT ON THE HOPE OF IMMORTALITY.

Immanuel Kant laughed bitterly at all ghost-seers, and considered Swedenborg only fit for an insane asylum. Speaking on the subject, he says:

"I do not know that there are spirits. What is more, I do not know what the word spirit means." Yet, elsewhere, he writes: "But, probably, never lived a righteous soul that could bear the thought that death is the end of all, and whose noble disposition did not rise to a hope of the future. Therefore, it seems more proper for human nature and for the purity of morals to base the expectation of a future world on the emotions of a good soul than, inversely, to base the goodness of the soul on the hope of another world."

LORD BYRON ON THE WHITE LADY OF COLALTO.

Fancy Lord Byron believing in a spectre—yet, he writes to Mr. Murray:

"The White Lady of Avernel is not quite so good as a real, well-authenticated Dona Bianca, White Lady of Colalto, who has been repeatedly seen. There is a man, a huntsman, now alive, who saw her. Hoppner could tell you all about her—Rose, also, perhaps.

"I, myself, have no doubt of the fact, historical or spectral.

"She always appeared on particular occasions, before the deaths in the family, etc., etc.

"I heard Madame Benzoni say that she knew a gentleman who had seen her cross his room at Colalto Castle.

"Hoppner saw and spoke to the huntsman who met her at the chase and never hunted afterward. She was a girl attendant, who, one day, dressing the hair of the Countess Colalto, was seen by her mistress to smile upon her husband, in the glass.

"The Countess had her shut up in the wall of the Castle, like Constance de Beverly—ever after she haunted them and all the Colaltos. She is described as very beautiful and fair. It is well authenticated."

The well-known story of Mozart's last Requiem is only occult in the very widest sense: for it is stated that the mysterious person who ordered the composition was afterward known to be a servant of Count Walsegg—one Leutgeb; but the positive certainty that Mozart felt that he was writing his own Requiem is none the less remarkable.

Another curious story was told by his young sister-in-law, who believed in omens. In the early morning, as she was preparing breakfast, a candle still remained burning. To quote her own words—"fixing my eyes steadily on the flame, I said—'I should like to know how Mozart is'—and, suddenly, as if in answer, the light went out as completely as if it had never been burning; not a spark was to be seen lingering on the thick wick, and I am quite positive that there was not the slightest current of air."

On this, she felt that an unfavorable answer had been given her, and hastened to Mozart's house, to find him dying.

MR. FRITH'S DREAM OF DICKENS.

It is stated on excellent authority, that the artist Frith, on rising on the morning of June 9th, 1870, said —"I dreamed last night that Charles Dickens was dead." A few moments later, news was brought him of the sad and sudden event.

VICTOR HUGO.

. Besides feeling that he knew the soul to be immortal, and hoping for greater opportunities after death than he ever had before, Victor Hugo went so far as to believe that a table spelled out words by raps without the assistance of the mind of any human being present. One or two seances, which he attended, made him declare that a medium was by no means certain to be a trickster—though he felt that there was something in all the mysteries of Spiritualism which made them unwholesome for men who wished to keep their own minds in good working order.

ABERCROMBIE'S OPINION.

Abercrombie says: "Our speculations respecting the immateriality of the rational human soul have no influence on our belief of its immortality. This momentous truth rests on a species of evidence altogether different, which addresses itself to the moral constitution of man. It is found in those principles of his nature by which he feels upon his spirit the awe of God, and looks forward to the future with anxiety or with hope—by which he knows to distinguish truth from falsehood and evil from good, and has forced upon him the conviction that he is a moral and responsible being. This is the power of conscience, that monitor within which raises its voice in the breast of every man, a witness for his Creator. He who resigns himself to its guidance, and he who repels its warnings, are both compelled to acknowledge its power, and, whether the good man rejoices in the prospect of immortality, or the victim of remorse withers beneath an influence unseen by human eye, and shrinks from the anticipation of a reckoning to come, each has forced upon him a conviction, such as argument never gave, that the being which is essentially himself is distinct from any function of the body, and will survive in undiminished vigor when the body has fallen into decay.

"When, indeed, we take into the inquiry the high principles of moral obligation, and the moral government of the deity, this important truth is altogether independent of all our feeble speculations on the essence of mind. For, though we were to suppose, with the materialist, that the rational soul of man is a mere chymical combination, which, by the dissolution of its elements, is dissipated to the four winds of Heaven, where is the improbability that the power which framed the wondrous compound may collect these elements again and combine them anew, for the great purposes of his moral administration? In our speculations on such a momentous subject we are too apt to be influenced by our perceptions of the powers and properties of physical things; but there is a point where this principle must be abandoned, and where the soundest philosophy requires that we take along with us a full recognizance of the power of God.

"There is thus, in the consciousness of every man, a deep impression of continued existence. The casuist may reason against it till he bewilder himself in his own sophistries, but a voice within gives the lie to his vain speculations, and pleads with authority for a life which is to come. The sincere and humble inquirer cherishes the impression, while he seeks for further light on a subject so momentous; and he thus receives, with absolute conviction, the truth which beams upon him from the revelation of God—that the mysterious part of his being, which thinks, and wills, and reasons, shall, indeed, survive the wreck of its mortal tenement, and is destined for immortality."

A BEAUTIFUL HOPE OF THE THOSEOPHIST.

Theosophists, while they believe in the intercommunication of the spirit of the living man with that of disembodied personalities, say that it is not the spirits of the dead who come to earth, but the spirits of the living that go to meet the pure spiritual souls in their higher state. That, in this way, those who really attract each other spiritually, can and do communicate, generally in a dream—which is not all a dream—which in some sensitively organized people becomes a trance.

Madame Blavatsky says—"although there is hardly a human being who does not hold free intercourse, during the sleep of his body, with those whom it has loved and lost, yet, on account of the positiveness and non-receptivity of its physical envelope and brain, no recollection, or only a very dim, fleeting remembrance, lingers in the memory of the person once awake."

Theosophists believe, too, that, for a very brief period, the real *ego* may remain on earth, and has occasionally communicated with those to whom it intensely desired to speak—then it becomes unconscious and awakes in Devachan.

For ten or fifteen centuries, the spirit, worn out with the trials of life, is permitted to rest in that heavenly place, whence all woe is banished, where the best and most blissful part of life is repeated, without the shadows which memory and anxiety for the future cast upon us here. And though they believe that a soul is not made for each body, but that our souls return to earth many times, they declare that spiritual holy love is immortal, and that those who have loved each other with true affection will incarnate again in the same family group; for, to quote H. P. B. again, "Pure, divine love is not merely the blossom of the human heart, but has its roots in eternity."

HERBERT SPENCER.

Herbert Spencer says: "Whatever doctrine or opinion has received, through a long succession of centuries, the common assent of mankind may be properly set down as being, if not absolutely true in its usually received form, yet founded on truth, and having, at least, a great undeniable verity that underlies it.

"If, however, there be conflicting details as to any doctrine, varying in form according to the sect or the nation that entertains it, then the test is to be received as affirming the grand underlying truth, but not as proving any of the conflicting varieties of investment in which particular sects or nations may have chosen to clothe it."

Thus of the world's belief in the reality of another life and in the doctrine of future reward and punishment. In some form or other, such a faith has existed in every age and among almost every people.

The Fathers of the Church regarded dreams as revelations from God, and the tales they tell are very wonderful. They also believed that some dreams were from Satan.

St. Augustine declares that some very practical and sensible advice as to worldly matters has been given in these devils' dreams, but probably there was an evil intention at the bottom of this seeming amiability.

Both this saint and St. Chrysostom could distinguish between devils' dreams and God-given dreams.

Bishop Ken, pious man, wrote on the subject. He believed that dreams were from God himself—a revelation of divine mercy.

Here is a quotation from him:

"I, waking, called my dream to mind,
Which, to instruct me, Heaven designed."

The Divina Comedia was partially inspired by a dream.

A bishop of Gloucester gives evidence that one Mrs. Greenwood dreamed of a murder, all its incidents, and the names of those concerned—not in one dream, but five. The people were strangers to her. Knowing nothing but what she saw in her dreams, she acted as detective in the case, each dream indicating some special point in the case, and showing where one of the several murderers might be found. Full confession was made, and her dreams were true in every particular.

EXTRACTS FROM HAWTHORNE'S NOTE-BOOKS.

ON A HAPPY ANNIVERSARY, SUNDAY, JULY 9TH.

"God bless and keep us! For there is something more awful in happiness than in sorrow—the latter being earthly and finite, the former composed of the substance and texture of eternity, so that spirits still embodied may well tremble at it."

ON A BRIGHT DAY.

"Oh, perfect day! Oh, beautiful world! Oh, good God! And such a day is the promise of a blissful eternity.

"Our Creator would never have made such weather, and given us the deep heart to enjoy it, above and beyond all thought, if he had not meant us to be immortal. It opens the gates of Heaven and gives us glimpses far inward."

In another place, Hawthorne mentions sitting with his friends, Emerson and Margaret Fuller, telling ghost-stories until midnight, which proved that such tales were not utterly contemptible in the eyes of any of the three.

CHAPTER 19.

THE HAUNTED HEARTH.

For the story which follows, I am indebted to one who was well acquainted with the lady to whom the occult manifestations occurred, and is personally aware that all happened as it is told.

It is now many years since an elderly lady, who had recently become a resident of ———, hired of its owner an old-fashioned house which had not been occupied for some time, and, having apportioned certain rooms to the various members of her family, reserved for herself one which had a wide fire-place and a low mantel-piece. In this she kept a good fire all the time, and was in the habit of toasting herself thoroughly at it just before retiring.

Now, there are in this world—let who will deny it—certain people who are subject to psychical impressions—this lady was one. No sooner had she settled herself in her room than she became aware that, whenever she stood upon the hearth, before the fire, leaning upon the low, wooden mantel-piece, as was her wont, a sense of horror fell upon her—not a presentiment, but a sort of shadow of the past. Something seemed to whisper to her: "There has been a tragedy enacted here—just here—upon this hearth—in the light of such a fire as this."

She became, after awhile, perfectly certain that this was so. Daily, the impression grew stronger, and at last, in the solemn silence of a winter midnight, a picture grew before her eyes.

Just how or whence these pictures come, or even how they are seen, mortal lips have no power to say, but the picture was there, and it was this:

The fire blazed high upon the andirons; there was no light in the room but that which it gave, glowing red against the black chimney-back, flinging vermil touches upon the walls, golden glints upon the ceiling, touching the dusky drapery of the bed and curtain here and there.

Before the fire, upon the rug, sat a man and woman, locked in each other's arms—lovers, whose lips met. Suddenly, a third figure joined the group—the scene became one of hideous conflict and confusion. Then the two lovers lay pallid, blood-stained—dead upon the hearth—and the third figure was gone. A moment the ghastly forms of his victims remained, then the vision faded utterly.

Having had previous experiences, the lady who had witnessed all this felt certain that such a tragedy as had been presented to her had really been enacted in that house; but, not being acquainted with her neighbors, spoke to no one on the subject.

As to the old house, she knew nothing of its history, having never seen it before the day on which she resolved to live there.

After the night of the vision, I believe, she had no more unusual experiences.

A few months later, having occasion to hire a new servant, she was told of an old colored woman who was desirous of finding a place, and sent for her.

Old Aunt Polly, as I will call her, presented herself very shortly. She wanted work and was satisfied with the offer made her, but evidently there was something on her mind. She rolled her head about, looked down at the floor and up at the ceiling, and, finally, made her speech. It was to the effect that, much as she desired to make the engagement, she could not come to the house unless she received assurance that she should never be sent into a certain room. "Not to make de fire, nor sweep de floor, nor make up de bed, nor nuffin, missus," she went on. "I cyant come, no ways, ef I is to be sent into dat yar room—wid de big fire-place, and de great harf, an de low ceilin';" and she went on to describe the room in which the mistress of the mansion had seen the vision of the murder. "Perhaps that could be managed," the lady told her; but she must give a good reason for the request.

"Oh, yas'm," Polly replied, "dar is good reasons—murder was done in dat yar room, and dar is haants dar, sartin shore.

"Folks has seen 'em, everybody knows de room is haanted." Then she proceeded to tell her tale:

Twenty years before, a very unhappy couple had inhabited that house. They quarreled incessantly, and, moreover, the husband was jealous. At first only vaguely, but at last suspicion deepened to certainty, and he became positive that, during his frequent absences from home, his wife entertained a lover. Whether he had received private information, or employed any spy, will never be known; but, suddenly, he seemed to abandon his suspicions, to grow trustful and affectionate, and, finally, made arrangements for a long journey—told his wife that he would be away many weeks—and bade her a tender farewell.

This, however, was only a plan to entrap her. He had so arranged matters that he could enter the house at any time, and he remained where he could watch her movements.

The traitress was completely deceived, and her lover entered the house that very night as soon as the shadows were deep enough to hide him from the eyes of the neighbors.

A little later, the injured master of the house opened the door of his desecrated home, and noiselessly made his way to that low-ceiled room with the wide fire-place, which I have described.

Secure in her freedom from observation, the adulteress had not even locked the door. There were no servants, no children in the house, no one but herself and the partner of her unholy love, and these two sat on the great rug before the hearth, folded in each other's arms, when the outraged husband suddenly stood beside them. He slew them both, but not without a fierce struggle with the man (who lived long enough to tell the truth), and then stalked out of the house, and went, whither no one knew—he was never seen, never heard of again.

"Sence dat yar night," Aunt Polly said, "dey walks; nobody kin lib in dat yar room; dey skeers em so."

"Was the woman a little, slender creature, with a thin face and big owl-eyes?" the lady asked.

"Yes'm," replied Aunt Polly; "she did look jes dat way, sartin shore."

The lady then described the two men whom she had seen in her vision, and Aunt Polly cried out:

"Why, you must have knowed 'em! Dat is jes like dey all looked."

But Mrs. —— had only recently arrived in the place, and had never before heard of any of these people, or even that a tragedy had occurred beneath the roof of the old house.

This is certainly one of the most singular of psychical stories, and it was told me by a person who would not utter falsehood.

SLEEPING-CAR DREAMS.

In the columns of the *Herald*, I find the tale that follows, reported by police officers and those who legally investigated the case:

A married woman, who resided in the city of San Francisco, having reason to complain of her husband, and desiring a divorce from him, instituted proceedings against him, and sent for her sister, who lived, I believe, in Ohio, asking her to come to her and give evidence which would assist her to gain her case.

The sister agreed to do so, and left her home for that purpose.

Before starting upon her journey, she took the precaution to conceal a sum of money (three thousand dollars, I believe) about her person. She did this by placing it in a small, linen bag, and stitching the bag neatly into the bosom of her corset, where its presence would never be suspected by strangers.

Having cash enough in her purse for all her needs, she was not obliged to undo her work, and as she saw, every night, that the little bag was where she had placed it, she had no anxiety as to the safety of the contents.

She remained in San Francisco until the case was settled and her sister obtained her divorce, and then left for home, never having examined the bag of money, which she had not spoken of to any one; but, while reposing in the sleeping-car, on the first night of her journey, she dreamed a dream.

In it her sister stole away her corset, ripped out the bag, took out a great portion of the money it contained, restored the remainder to its old place, and stitched the bag to the garment once more.

Awaking, she dismissed the whole thing as an absurd fancy, and went to sleep again; but, on arising in the morning, she felt that she would be easier after counting the money once more, and, having done so, found, to her horror, that the sum of which she had dreamed had actually been abstracted from the original quantity.

Her mind was made up at once. At the next station she alighted and returned to San Francisco, appeared before her sister without warning, and accused her of the theft.

The indignant denial that injured innocence might

have uttered was her reply; but she had her sister arrested and searched—the stolen money was found stitched into her dress. Confession followed, and the whole sum was restored.

The story ends there, a tragic little tale enough—if there had ever been any sisterly love between the two women—but yet another prophetic dream to add to the list already collected.

Another sleeping-car dream is that of a Mr. Frost, who dreamed of the particulars of an accident which happened several hours later. The cause of the trouble, the spot where it occurred, and the faces of the two men who were injured, had all been seen by him, though he attached no importance to his dream at the time.

Railroad employees frequently have presentiments of accidents. Engineers, more than once, have pointed out the spots where they were to meet their death, and where they did eventually meet it—and, on the day itself, have, without reason, declared that their time had come.

These premonitions might readily be explained by the fact that the lives of these men are continually in danger, and that any unusual depression will remind them of it; but they are, nevertheless, too well attested to be entirely set aside.

Many years have passed since the steamer Westfield, on her Sunday morning trip to Staten Island, burst her boiler just as she was leaving New York. It was a frightful affair, in which a number of people were scalded to death, many of them prominent persons.

I have heard a gentleman tell how he started that morning, in due season, to reach the fated boat—how, do what he might, delays occurred. He could not find his hat, his coat, his gloves, his shoes seemed to play hide and seek with him, his door seemed locked on the outside—then burst open and gave him a fall, scattering the contents of a portmanteau he carried, in all directions. On the steps of his house a neighbor buttonholed him, the car-conductors passed him at full speed, regardless of his signals. When he, finally, entered a car, he left it without taking his portmanteau, and was obliged to go to the office to claim his property, which had been carried thither.

Though usually light on his feet and not apt to blunder, he stumbled frequently and, once, fell down flat. His watch-chain caught in the fringe of a lady's mantle, and he was obliged to wait while she daintily picked away the silk with a hair-pin, in order not to injure it.

It seemed, he said, that a demon was tormenting him—but, with all this, he reached the wharf but an instant too late, and the angry oath which he was about to utter, had not left his lips, when the explosion occurred, and changed it to thanksgiving for his safety.

It then became his fixed conviction that his guardian-angel had been trying to save his life, while he resisted him. Why *his* particularly? one may ask, remembering all the innocent people who suffered and died, and those who mourned them, who were not less deserving of angelic protection. Still, his mishaps and detentions were exceptional.

CHAPTER 20.

MYSTERY STORIES.

The most astonishing of all the mysterious stories I have ever heard, are three in which living people vanish before the eyes of those who are gazing upon them, two to be seen no more.

All seem well-authenticated, though they pass the boundaries of human comprehension.

One is of an athlete who was competing in a foot-race with others, surrounded by a crowd of witnesses. One instant he was seen by all, the next he was gone, to the astonishment of the spectators, especially of the man behind him, who was looking at him as he vanished.

There was nothing but a clear track, barricaded as usual, and the crowd beyond it. All eyes were intent on the probable winner, when another man was seen to lead the race. Nothing was ever again known of the hero of this story.

Another case was that of a man who vanished at the door of his neighbor's house, in an American country-place.

Witnesses were called upon to testify to the fact, as there was a suspicion of foul play. People who had no interest in the matter declared that it was an actual case of vanishing from sight.

The third story was of a gentleman, who was apparently attacked by delirium, and begged his friends to lock him into a room and stay with him. They did so. Their eyes never left him. They believed him to be about to be attacked by serious illness; yet, suddenly, he was no longer with them. No door had been opened, no window, yet he was gone.

Three years afterward, they found him at the door of the same house—his own home. He was unconscious of having left it, remembered nothing of the interval, could not believe the time had passed, and was horrified by what they told him. Nor was he ever able to recall any event between the hour when he begged for protection from some invisible power which seemed to try to force him from his friends, until that when he heard them greet and question him. Nothing unusual ever occurred to him again.

THE SON RESTORED TO HIS MOTHER.

There is a French tale that caps these—told by a man of position, who dwelt, for a time, in the home of a poor peasant woman, his purpose being, I believe, to study the people of a certain place, of which he desired to write. Certainly, he had a strange experience.

While he dwelt there, the oldest son of the family—a fine fellow, on whom they all relied for support, and who was very kind and lovable—died suddenly. The grief of the relatives was terrible. Their guest grieved with them, and was present at the funeral and burial.

The mother and sisters bewailed the young man

wildly, and cried out that they could not live without him, they actually prayed that he might "return"—a mad prayer enough, but, according to their literary guest, it was granted. One day, the family found their lost brother in his bed, as of old.

They seemed to feel no great astonishment—their delight, however, was past bounds. Neighbors came in and welcomed him. The priest confessed that a miracle had occurred. He, himself, said that he had been to Heaven, but that he had been permitted to return because of the longing he felt to do so, and the prayers of his kindred. He was forbidden to describe what he had heard and seen, but told them that he was to be allowed to stay a certain number of years, until his mother should no longer need him—ten, I believe.

No one in the whole place doubted his identity, the distinguished guest least of all.

The story goes on to say that the young peasant lived exactly the length of time that he had mentioned, and passed away, following his mother, who died in his arms, very quickly. The closest particulars are given in the diary which used to be part of the earlier biographies of the author, who attests the facts.

The narrator of this story ends with words to this effect: "These facts have convinced me of what I never thought I should believe—that man possesses an immortal soul."

No doubt, friends and admirers of the author feared that his great reputation would suffer, and for this reason have suppressed the tale. About this time, too, it is said, he was attacked with brain-fever and threatened with insanity; and, as I conclude that this was the explanation of the whole thing, I do not use the well-known name of the dead author, who has a reputation as a great philosopher.

It is a pretty and tender story, however, with all that gentle beneficence about it which is the chief characteristic of French fairy tales. One might fancy Le Bon Dieu being thus merciful to those who appealed to him. I think every torn heart almost hopes for such sign of Heaven's pity when it is first crushed beneath a weight of woe; and there are stories like unto it in the New Testament, which all good Christians believe—this one, for instance:

ST. LUKE, CHAPTER VII.

12. Now, when Jesus came nigh to the gate of the city, behold, there was a dead man carried out, the only son of his mother, and she was a widow, and much people of the city was with her.

13. And when the Lord saw her, He had compassion on her, and said unto her, "Weep not."

14. And He came and touched the bier, and they that bare the dead man stood still, and Jesus said: "Young man, I say unto thee, arise."

15. And he that was dead sat up and began to speak, and Jesus delivered him to his mother. And there came a fear on all, and they glorified God.

And that other story of Lazarus, the brother of Mary and Martha, who had lain in the grave four days, when Jesus raised him.

Assuredly, if God ever took heed of the special needs and griefs of individuals, he may do so still.

It seems to you, and it seems to me, impossible that the young peasant should have been raised from the dead; but, after all, what do we know?

—— may have been mad, and in his madness imagined the exquisite story; but he printed the signature of the mayor of the place and of several important residents, attached to words something like this:

"To the best of our knowledge and belief, having personally known the dead man, who lived again amongst us after having been laid in his grave, this story is perfectly true; and God, in his mercy, has performed a great miracle."

I quote from memory.

www.ingramcontent.com/pod-product-compliance
Lightning Source LLC
Chambersburg PA
CBHW031739230426
43669CB00007B/404